To Merlin Forster

and thanks
for your
advice
— Naomi

LITERARY
EXPRESSIONISM
IN
ARGENTINA

LITERARY EXPRESSIONISM IN ARGENTINA:
THE PRESENTATION OF INCOHERENCE

By
Naomi Lindstrom

CENTER FOR LATIN AMERICAN STUDIES
ARIZONA STATE UNIVERSITY

LIBRARY OF CONGRESS CATALOGING IN PUBLICATION DATA

Lindstrom, Naomi, 1950-
    Literary expressionism in Argentina.

    Includes bibliographical references.
    1. Argentine literature--20th century--History
and criticism. 2. Expressionism. I. Title.
PQ7655.L5   860'.9   77-24558
ISBN 0-87918-038-2

To FBL and the tribe

ACKNOWLEDGMENTS

Preliminary versions of small portions of this study appeared in Romance Notes, Chasqui, Latin American Literary Review, and Kentucky Romance Quarterly.

TABLE OF CONTENTS

Chapter 1

Introduction

I

One of the most elusive goals of literary criticism
is the formulation of adequate general characterizations
of literary movements. Despite the lack of absolute definitions, there is a good deal of consensus on what constitute the chief characteristics of literary expressionism.
This general agreement allows one to identify and discuss
expressionism in works that were not considered expressionistic by their authors or by contemporary readers. In the
case of such works, one cannot demonstrate their expressionistic nature by citing such external evidence as the author's
announced adherence to the main tenets of expressionism or
his participation in the drafting of expressionist manifestos. The works themselves must reveal, upon examination,
the features of expressionistic writing.

This study must start by setting forth the principal
identifying features of expressionism because most of the
works it discusses are shown to be instances of "unannounced"
expressionism. Although, as we will see, Latin American
literary history was influenced by European expressionism,
most of the works here discussed were not held to be expressionistic at the time of publication. However, as is well
known, contemporary reaction to a work of literature may
rely more on extrinsic considerations and on superficial
characteristics of the work than on any thoughtful examination. A subsequent generation of readers and critics,
reading the same writings with new eyes, may question the
traditional classification and situate the work within an
entirely different literary current. A dramatic instance
of such a re-appraisal is provided by the case of Roberto
Arlt (1900-42), one of the authors this study will discuss.

The typical contemporary reaction to Arlt's fiction
was aptly caricatured by the author himself: "El señor Arlt
persiste aferrado a su realismo de pésimo gusto."[1] Con-
temporaries saw Arlt's writings as an attempt to transcribe
societal realities directly onto the page, unmediated by
the author's poetic imagination. It is easy to see the
surface resemblance between Arlt's work and documentary
realism. Arlt's themes often coincide with those of the
realist: social unrest, deviant behavior, anomie among
urban dwellers, marginal individuals, sexual maladjustment
and class hostilities. The novels abound in pimps, prostitutes, gamblers and the poorest of the urban poor.
Scabrous incidents and profanity occur with great frequency.
Moreover, Arlt's Spanish deviates to an often startling
extent from prevailing academic, literary standards. His
mode of expression was deviant enough not only to classify
him as an ostensible realist, but also to make readers
"encoger los hombros y rezongar piadosamente que Arlt no
sabía escribir,"[2] as Juan Carlos Onetti described this
reaction.

Extrinsic considerations tended to support the notion
that Arlt was attempting the most direct realism. The
writers with whom he associated himself sought to make
literature more accessible by minimizing the intervention
of the literary imagination. Jean Franco summarizes: "in
the 1920s the *Boedo* group who admired Gorky, were vocal
in their insistence that art should not be the province of
an elite. *Boedo* counted in its ranks many intelligent and
dedicated novelists, including Alvaro Yunque (b. 1890),
Roberto Mariani (1893-1945), Elias Castelnuovo (b. 1893),
Max Dickman (b. 1902), Lorenzo Stanchina (b. 1900) and
Roberto Arlt (1900-1942)."[3] Statements by Arlt presented
his work as writing devoid of literary effects: "entre
las ruinas de un mundo social que se desmorona inevitable-
mente, no es posible pensar en bordados."[4] If one classified Arlt's writing purely on the basis of the introductory
remarks, he could easily imagine it to be closer to immediate reportage than to literature in the usual sense.
     However, this facile classification does not hold up
when one reads the works themselves. By 1968 the reexam-
ination of Arlt's writing had discovered elements of
fantasy, of imaginative distortion--in short, evidence of
a representation of reality that was not doggedly mimetic
but decidedly expressionistic, not a literal transcription
of reality but rather a highly figurative representation.
In that year Adolfo Prieto wrote: "Es cierto que la mención de Roberto Arlt en un análisis específico de la literatura fantástica puede parecer extravagante, tanto pesa la
imagen del creador de *El juguete rabioso,* realista pertinaz
y hasta obseso, testigo del mundo apasionado e insobornable.
Pero basta releer sus obras, sin la presión de esa imagen,
para empezar a admitir que por debajo, o junto con la
indiscutible voluntad del realismo, Arlt alimentaba una
fuerte tendencia a manifestarse con fórmulas en las que
la fantasía juega alucinantes contrapuntos con la experiencia de lo real."[5] Prieto urges readers to look beyond the
features that give Arlt's work "la imprenta de un verismo
desgarrador."[6]
     Indeed, since the sixties Arltian criticism has been
increasingly focused on imaginative and poetic elements.
Noé Jitrik, for instance, counts Arlt among the writers
who bridged the gap in Argentine letters between the artless and direct on the one hand and the purposefully and
intentionally "literary" on the other: "estos puentes se
hacen cada vez más frecuentes, y en escritores como Benito
Lynch, Macedonio Fernández, Horacio Quiroga, Roberto Arlt,
las dos líneas se entremezclan tanto que casi podríamos
hablar de una síntesis, de una naturalidad que combina sin
violencia cultura y populismo, nacionalismo y extranjerismo,
en suma legitimidad con representividad."[7] Jitrik considers
"el famoso escribir mal de Roberto Arlt" as a deliberate
literary choice, a purposeful challenge to prevailing norms,
rather than an accident.[8]
     Almost as dramatic as the reevaluation of Arlt is that
of the dramatist Armando Discépolo (1887), another representative of Argentine expressionism. Like Arlt, Discépolo
had been relegated to a category far from expressionism, in
the latter's case, *costumbrismo.* David Viñas, though, pref-
aced his 1969 edition of Discépolo's *Obras escogidas* with
an essay presenting the playwright not as a master of local

color, but rather as a practitioner of international
expressionism.[9] Another Viñas essay, "El escritor
vacilante: Arlt, Boedo y Discépolo," examines works
long held to be realistic and finds the magical, the
poetic, the imaginative and the metaphorical. What is
most notable is his emphasis on these expressionistic
features in the writings of authors considered the most
doggedly literal transcribers of social realities.[10]
Again, writings that do not announce themselves as expressionistic reveal, upon examination, the most undeniable
features of literary expressionism.

II

Although this study deals mainly with "unannounced"
manifestations of expressionism, there is evidence that
international--and particularly German--expressionism did
have a significant impact on Latin American literary history. True, there is no Spanish American equivalent of
the many manifestos and programmatic statements issued by
the German expressionists. While historians of German
literature can cite, for instance, Kasimir Edschmid's
"Über den Expressionismus in der Literatur und die neue
Dichtung" or point to group efforts by the Menschheitsdämmerung poets, self-announced expressionists, such open
avowals of expressionism are lacking in Latin America.
However, it is evident that the main principles of German
expressionism traveled to Buenos Aires, in particular, and
made an impact on Latin American literature in this way.
German expressionism, the self-proclaimed innovative
movement, was the model for the unannounced but yet evident Latin American equivalent.

Jorge Luis Borges (b.1899) is particularly important as
a means of transmission for the works, themes, techniques
and ideas of German expressionism. It is well known that
Borges spent his formative years in Europe and as a young
poet read the expressionists in German. Overwhelmed by
their innovations, he attempted to reproduce their fragmented syntax and horrors-of-war theme in Spanish. The
resulting verses, published only in 1964, exhibit the
features of literary expressionism. However, their limited
merit as poetry relegates them to the status of museum
pieces. They do constitute perhaps the most overt case of
cause-and-effect in the transmission of expressionism from
Germany to Latin America.[11]

Despite this false start, Borges's literary career
has been enriched by his knowledge of the German expressionists. One has only to look through Borges's writings
to note a profusion of references to German expressionist
works. The 1964 poem "El Golem," by presupposing some
familiarity with Gustav Meyrinck's 1915 novel *Der Golem,*
reminds the reader that he ought to be able to place this
key work of expressionism.[12] Borges undertook the trans-
lation of Kafka into Spanish and brought Kafka and other
expressionists to the attention of the Spanish-reading
public through lectures and essays like the 1952 "Kafka y
sus precursores."[13] His championing of the German expressionists makes him an important link between the German
movement and its Latin American counterpart.

Another connecting figure is Ramón Gómez de la Serna (1888-1963), the avant-garde Spanish writer who emigrated to Buenos Aires in 1936. The name of Gómez de la Serna has been linked to many of the vanguardistic movements that shook European culture early in the century. Rodolfo Cardona states that Gómez de la Serna "manifested his concern with the problems posed by the main literary and artistic currents of our century. Not only do we find in his works attitudes, themes, ideas and styles which one would ordinarily connect with the 'isms' of the twentieth century, but in most cases he seems to have heralded these attitudes, these themes, these ideas and these styles."[14] Gómez de la Serna lectured all over Europe, conversed with the emblematic figures of *entreguerre* cultural innovation and ran a *tertulia* that attracted such luminaries as Pablo Neruda, Tristan Tzara and Karl Vossler. Rita Mazzatti Gardiol states that Gómez de la Serna influenced José Ortega y Gasset in discussions on alternatives to mimetic art.[15]

When the Civil War forced Gómez de la Serna to flee to Argentina, he maintained his role as catalyst for cultural innovation. His entry into the country was facilitated by the P.E.N. Club, and he immediately became active on the Buenos Aires literary scene. He wrote journalism, lectured, spoke at literary banquets and published nearly all his books with Argentine publishers. Among the founders of the innovative magazine *Sur* appears the name of Ramón Gómez de la Serna.[16] The Spaniard maintained a long correspondence with the Argentine expressionist writer Macedonio Fernández (1874-1952) on the evolution of artistic expression.[17] Even the "realist" Arlt recommends to readers of his newspaper column the writings of Ramon Gomez de la Serna, a fact that points obliquely to the expressionistic nature of Arlt's own work.[18] The total effect of Gómez de la Serna's involvement in Argentine letters was to move writers away from traditional realism and toward more metaphorical, fanciful representations of the world.

Thus, literary history would seem to situate Latin American expressionism chiefly in Buenos Aires. Such may well be the case, and, in fact, the Argentine capital would be a logical focal point for the *entreguerre* literary movement. During the expressionist years--roughly 1915-40--Latin America boasted two real literary capitals, Buenos Aires and Mexico City. Mexico's literary climate, though, was characterized by concentration on national authors and specifically Mexican subject matter. Correspondingly, the literary life of Mexico City displayed a less international character, less receptivity to currents from abroad and fewer parallels to what was happening in world literature. The poets associated with the famous magazine *Contemporáneos* (1928-31) marked the beginning of the gradual incorporation of Mexican literature into world literature.

Argentina, though, showed keen interest in European literary trends. Both those who considered this receptivity to European innovations a sign of awareness and sophistication and those who decried its intensity recognized the importance of foreign influences in the history of Argentine literature. It was this European orientation which allowed Gómez de la Serna, immigrating under the

aegis of the Argentine P.E.N. Club, to resume his literary
career upon arrival in Buenos Aires.

The idea that one ought to find inspiration in European
culture impelled many Argentines to travel or reside in
Europe. Adolfo Prieto notes of the "uncultured" Arlt:
"lo que es muy curioso, indica ilustres antecedentes de la
literatura universal: 'los espantables personajes que
animan el drama (*El fabricante de fantasmas,* 1936) son una
reminiscencia de mi recorrido por los museos españoles:
Goya, Durero y Breughel el Viejo, quien con sus farsas de
la Locura y de la Muerte reactivaron en mi sentido teatral
la afición a lo maravilloso que hoy, insisto nuevamente,
se atribuye con excesiva ligereza a la influencia de
Pirandello, como si no existieran los previos antecedentes
de la actuación de la fantasmagoría en Calderón de la
Barca, Shakespeare y Goethe'."[19]   Arlt's remarks here
remind one of the German interest in finding and rereading
the precursors of expressionism. René Wellek has described
the vogue for "literature whose beauties were discovered
during the change of taste caused by expressionism."[20]

A writer living in Buenos Aires between the wars was
no isolated toiler, then, but rather an inhabitant of a
city attuned to European culture and its proliferation of
" isms." Arlt, while maintaining an uncultured image, was
neither unread nor untraveled. He spent a year observing
and commenting upon the Spanish scene for the newspaper
El Mundo.[21]   His journalistic notes, reprinted in book
form, abound in references to literature and European culture, confirming Prieto's skepticism about Arlt's fabled
semiliteracy. Both Borges and Macedonio Fernández won fame
for their mastery of vast reserves of cultural data from
wide-ranging sources. Both assimilated their knowledge
about literature and philosophy through eclectic readings
and conversations with urbane, clever people whose cultural
knowledge was quite current.

Argentine expressionists did not, of course, join in
proclaiming themselves a movement. However, the various
expressionistic writers seem to have been aware of one
anothers' innovations. Jorge Luis Borges has always pro-
claimed his debt to Macedonio Fernández: "Yo por aquellos
anos lo imité, hasta la transcripción, hasta el apasionado
y devoto plagio. Yo sentía: Macedonio *es* la metafísica,
es la literatura."[22]   The exchange of letters between Macedonio Fernández and Ramón Gómez de la Serna antedates the
latter's move to Buenos Aires. The two correspondents
clearly thought of their exchange as part of the search
for nonmimetic forms of expression.[23]

Naturally it is difficult to find such acknowledge-
ments in the writings of Arlt, "cuyo programa literario...
excluía notoriamente toda vinculación con precursores,"[24]
as Prieto puts it. The "proletarian" author could hardly
refer his readers to the writings of authors like Borges,
associated with an elitist concept of literature. However,
Arlt does speak well of writers who were expressionistic
without having an elitist image. He calls Gómez de la
Serna's efforts "geniales,"[25] praises Armando Discépolo[26]
and speaks kindly of the Uruguayan Horacio Quiroga (1878-
1937). It is indicative of Arlt's expressionistic orientation that he situates Quiroga not among the world's

naturalist or realist writers, but rather in an imaginative, bizarre tradition: "Villiers de L'Isle Adam o Barbey
de Aurevilly o el barbudo de Horacio Quiroga."[27] Thus,
Arlt embraces the expressionistic efforts of his contem-
poraries so long as they are not tainted with elitism.
      Instead of a self-proclaimed movement, then, Argentine
expressionism took the form of innovative writings produced
in a literary climate favorable to experimentation with
nonmimetic literature. The main tenets of expressionism,
transmitted by such international literati as Borges and
Gómez de la Serna, won adherents among both writers associated with a cultural elite and those considered "proletarian." Indeed, the practice of dividing Argentine writers
of 1915-40 into cultivated men of letters and crude truth-
tellers may well have delayed the recognition of Argentine
expressionism as a phenomenon. Recently such critics as
Noé Jitrik[28] and David Viñas[29] have questioned the applicability of the categories mentioned above to Argentine literature of the expressionist period. To those who would
object that this study deals with writers too disparate to
be examined jointly, we can only reply that our focus is
on the features these writers have in common, not on those
that separate them. It is the features that these writers
have in common that make them expressionists and therefore
subject to discussion in a study on literary expressionism.

III

      How, then, does one determine what features charac-
terize Argentine expressionism? The features this study
will use must satisfy on two counts. First, they must be
characteristics which clearly appear in actual Latin American literary works of the 1915-40 period. Second, they
must also be traits of German expressionism, which is,
after all, the *fontis ab qua* the Argentine movement flows.
If someone were to demonstrate a basic, thoroughgoing lack
of correspondence between German expressionism and the
efforts of innovative Argentine writers of the twenties
and thirties, then the New World movement could not legit-
imately be called expressionism. Thus, this study must
refer back to generally-accepted and frequently-reiterated
distinguishing traits of German expressionism.
      Yet, one has only to begin to read characterizations
of the German movement to note that not all the discussion
is germane to the case of Argentine expressionism. Much
of what is said about the German movement is too specific
to Germany between the wars. A common practice is that of
finding parallels between literary manifestations of expressionism and other aspects of German life: the political
arena, the impact of philosophical ideas on the contemporary
layman, economic anxieties, "Weimar Culture" and radical
changes in mores.
      The authors of such studies seek to situate expres-
sionism within its native social context and thus to understand better both the literary-artistic movement and the
society that fostered it. An extreme instance is Siegfried
Kracauer's *From Caligari to Hitler,* which sees in expressionist films a reflection of the attitudinal changes that
led to the Third Reich.[30] Less unidimensional is Walter

H. Sokel's *The Writer in Extremis,* an examination of German
expressionism that focuses on the relations between writer
and society during the expressionist period in Germany.[31]
Most writers on German expressionism refer somewhat to its
societal context, as indicated by the very title of a general overview: *Expressionism in German Life, Literature
and the Theatre.*[32]

Undeniably, certain aspects of German expressionism
are specific to German literary and cultural history. Among
these are the formation of expressionist groups, the issuing
of manifestos and proclamations, Pinthus's famed anthology
of *Menschheitsdämmerung* poets, the spectacular theatrical
productions of expressionist dramas, the scandals provoked
by various prominent expressionists and the reaction of
the German public to all the above. However, the more significant facets of expressionism can be separated from the
circumstances under which the movement arose and flourished
in its homeland.

Moreover, nobody could be more insistent than the
expressionists themselves that their efforts were international, not culture- or nation-bound. Expressionism
sought to transcend national boundaries in order to address
itself to mankind as a whole, divested of its regional
peculiarities. As a history of the movement notes, "a poet
like Werfel will declare that all mankind is his brother,
hailing man as 'O Mensch!' And the minor dramatist Paul
Kornfeld asserts: 'Jeder Mensch ist ausserwählt'--a cheerful
if somewhat beery sentiment."[33] Viñas characterizes
Discépolo as expressionist rather than *costumbrista,* largely
because in that dramatist's works elements of local color
are subordinated to those of universal significance.[34]
Therefore, the most essential features of expressionism
must be applicable to its manifestations in any country's
literature.

The main tenets of international expressionism, as
they emerge from the proclamations of its originators and
the retrospective examination of their works by critics,
can be formulated in many ways. This study will concen-
trate on three features of the movement which seem both
frequently cited in discussions of German expressionism
and particularly salient in the works of Argentine expressionists. They are: 1) the use of literature to show man
the folly of trusting too fully in reason, science and in
literature with scientific pretensions; 2) the chaotic
structuring of literary work so as to impress upon the
reader the homologous disorder of the world in which he
lives; 3) the creation of fictional characters who are not
measurable against the real world as we can observe it,
and who are, in Mirta Arlt's words, "máscaras expresion-
istas"[35] rather than characters in the traditional sense.
Each of these categories will be discussed in more detail
at the beginning of the section dedicated to it.

It is apparent that these three aspects of expressionism have certain elements in common and do not constitute
entirely separate categories. For instance, the rejection
of "scientific" naturalism, the fashioning of a perplex-
ingly disordered narrative and the creation of inverisimilar
characters all manifest a distaste for the too-direct representation of reality in art. Expressionism held that art

must reflect life only in a metaphorical, indirect fashion,
mediated by poetic imagination. In the memorable words of
Kasimir Edschmid: "Die Welt ist da. Es wäre sinnlos, sie
zu wiederholen."[36] Kurt Pinthus specified that expressionism
"avoids naturalistic description of reality...; rather it
produces its means of expression with mighty, violent energy
from the...power of the spirit itself."[37] Edschmid, expressing in metaphorical fashion the expressionists' search for
highly metaphorical expression, stated that "They did not
look. They envisioned. They did not photograph. They had
visions."[38] David W. Foster summarizes: "Literary expressionism of the twenties and thirties is part of the attempt
to provide an alternative to Realism and Naturalism. In the
novel, the genre which best typifies realism, Expressionism
assumes the form of an *expression* more symbolic than anything
else. In place of the working-out of fictional contexts that
could be measured against observable reality, one finds
creative visions that were verisimilar only in the most
enigmatic of fashions."[39]
     Closely allied to the rejection of literal representa-
tion is the rejection of order and clarity as artistic goals.
One of the main tenets of expressionism was that human experience could not be tidily schematized, rationalized or
otherwise set in order. Man was an irrational creature who
found fulfillment or unhappiness through spiritual processes
not amenable to logical analysis or orderly enumeration and
description. Therefore, the artist must not falsify that
human experience by forcing it into a coherent fictional
scheme. For this reason one historian of German literature
titles his discussion of expressionism "Coherence Gone."[40]
Rational discourse and well-ordered exposition were super-
seded by the expressionistic *Schrei,* to use a contemporary
catchword for this disordered mode of expression. An extreme
instance of this disregard for coherence is the theater of
such dramatists as Reinhard Johannes Sorge (1892-1916). A
commentary warns that in Sorge's 1912 *Der Bettler* "The distri-
bution of the subject matter lacks any semblance of unity...
it is impossible to speak of a plot in *Der Bettler* in the
traditional sense. There are several motifs, all vaguely
connected and providing the basis for a certain amount of
action."[41] Another critic complains of the dramatist Carl
Sternheim (1878-1942): "as in the case of his Expressionist
friends, his total picture of society was confused; his heroes
lost themselves and the audience in labyrinths of meditation,
leaving the audience with no clear idea of what the author
imagined the future to hold for his characters or for them."[42]
     The reader of such disordered works or the spectator
of such chaotic dramas faces an arduous task. He may fault
the work for not complying with readerly demands for sufficient narrative data, an accessible scheme of ideas, characters with recognizable identities and a plot that makes
sense. This study, however, will try to follow Wolfgang
Kayser's injunction to critics: "La negligencia frente a
la unidad de acción y la ausencia de una estructuracíon
rígida ha de entenderse mediante una interpretacion positiva
de la esencia de cada drama, ya se trate de Gil Vicente o
de Hans Sachs, ya del drama español o de los representantes
del Sturm und Drang, de los románticos o de los expresion-
istas."[43] Kayser himself carefully points out the esthetic

principles that underlie and justify even the most disordered expressionist writings. Avoiding explanations
such as haste, illiteracy or madness on the part of the
author, Kayser reminds us that "La lucha contra todas las
reglas de gramática y contra la tradición terminó, por fin,
con el expresionismo, en una rotura de todos los vínculos
lingüísticos y en un balbuceo que ya no era lengua."[44]
Critics of Argentine expressionist writings would do
well to bear Kayser's words in mind. Arltian criticism
in particular has been quick to ascribe that writer's most
expressionistic features to his poor education, speed of
composition or personality disorganization.[45] Arlt himself
seems to have relished such *ad hoc* explanations, for he
made use of them. The dedication to *El criador de gorilas*
(1941) states that Arlt would have liked to write a cheerful work, but that the human distress he witnessed during
the gestation of the work left its mark on the stories con-
tained in it.[46] The introduction to *Los lanzallamas* contains
an elaborate description of Arlt's working conditions, given
as justification for his deviant mode of expression.[47]
Yet, to think of Arlt as the frustrated writer of sym-
metrical, polished novels on pleasant themes is neither
reasonable nor critically very productive. Recent Arlt
criticism represents a move away from biographical and
genetic explanations and toward seeing Arlt's linguistic
and structural aberrance as a purposeful literary device.
Jitrik, for instance, writes that in Arlt's generation "La
tendencia al realismo como denuncia, en cambio, al poner
en cuestión lo consolidado, instrumentaliza la palabra y
se margina voluntariamente de normas, echa mano a cualquier
recurso para lograr su objetivo: es el famoso escribir
mal de Roberto Arlt...."[48] Juan Carlos Onetti also views
Arlt's chaotic writing as a rejection of, rather than a
failure to meet, established norms: "desdeñaba el idioma
de los mandarines; pero sí dominaba la lengua y los
problemas de millones de argentinos, incapaces de comentar-
los en artículos literarios."[49] This study, then, will try
to provide the "interpretación positiva" that Kayser demands of criticism dealing with purposefully aberrant
works.

IV

The basis on which the present discussion of expressionism is delimited and circumscribed still needs clarification. Do the features chosen to typify literary
expressionism imply that the movement is essentially
thematic or structural in focus?
The major tenets of expressionism manifest themselves
both thematically and structurally. Expressionism presents
the world as a place unamenable to rational analysis, to
orderly classification and to scientifically accurate
description. Homologous to this untidy, ungraspable world
is the form of the literary work itself, disordered and
confusing to the reader. Just as the world is not constructed in a reasonable manner and man fails in his
attempts to understand it by clear thinking, the literary
work is not fashioned in a well-ordered, tidy way. The
work of literature refuses to give out a clear picture of

what is happening, as in the case of Sternheim's dramatic
works. But this apparent slovenly workmanship is purposeful, for the reader or spectator is made to recognize in
the chaos of the literary work the image of his own universe.

Thus in the works of Argentine expressionists we find
manifestations of this antirational, antiscientific spirit
both at a thematic and at a structural level. In Arlt's
Los lanzallamas (1931), for instance, the hero's infatua-
tion with science and technology often makes him behave in
a wrongheaded fashion. He allows himself to be lured into
criminal schemes by a shrewd charlatan who promises him
laboratories and a position as Head of Industries in a new
society. Thus his belief in science makes him weaker and
more fatuous than the charlatan, a thoroughgoing irrationalist. In this sense, the novel makes sport of man's
scientific aspirations on an essentially thematic level.

However, the construction of the novel also constitutes
a blow against science, reason, order and logic. The narrative is so structured as to frustrate the reader who demands
one rigorously accurate version of how matters stood. The
charlatan, for instance, may or may not have been capable of
implementing his scheme for a social revolution. His thesis
that well-planned mass deception can heal mankind's spiritual wounds may or may not be a valid one. The reader will
never know, because events disrupt the revolutionary gang
before it can undertake any actions. While the reader
searches in vain for some indication of the revolutionaries'
competence, the novel mocks and frustrates this quest for
definitive, objective truths. There is no reliable narrative voice that can be trusted to explain ambiguous points.
Instead, the reader must make his way through a bewildering
welter of unassimilable information. Included in *Los lanzallamas* are the plans for a poison-gas factory, several long
discussions of the logistics of the revolution, the interior monologues of several conspirators and some instances
of the leader's chaotic political discourse. The reader
may learn something of the spiritual meaning the conspiracy
has to each of its participants. But he cannot obtain even
the barest "objective" characterization; he does not know
if it was fascist or communistic, feasible or unworkable,
whether its leader meant to carry it out or keep it in the
realm of fantasy, whether its members were altruistic or
opportunistic.

Thus, the experience of the reader confronting the
work is that of man confronting a universe not amenable
to rational explanation. The fictional characters and
situations cannot be assigned objective characteristics,
because one has little "hard data" about them. Only the
irrational aspects of the conspiracy, its power to give
meaning to the spiritual lives of those involved, can be
known. The novel, like the expressionistic universe, is
riddled with ambiguities, anomalies, paradoxes and phenomena that defy clear explication. Both the literary work
and the universe are so constructed as to prevent man from
obtaining an objectively true, scientifically valid view
of all matters.

Thus, the structural aspects of expressionism reinforce the thematic ones and second the statements made at
a thematic level. For instance, in Discépolo's 1910

Entre el hierro, the applicability of reason to human behavior is debated by the characters. One asserts that
"Todo se consigue con lógica y con voluntad,"[50] while another
despairs of ratiocination. As the play progresses, the
usefulness of reason is questioned by the very structure
of the work. The spectator cannot abstract a clear picture
of the characters, their motives or the key events in their
pasts. A young woman marries a man unworthy of her. Of
the various, often conflicting explanations offered for her
actions, none emerges as the key to understanding her. For
instance, one character asserts that a deathbed promise
binds the couple, while another states that such promises
have no validity; neither is proven right or wrong. The
spectator is blocked in his attempts to reconstruct rationally the causes of the characters' present misery. His
frustration parallels that of the heroine who, urged to
confront her life with reason, declares herself weary of
ratiocination. "El frío de la comprensión es lo que me
sobra,"[51] she says, thus alerting the spectator to the
other-than-rational nature of the expressionistic world
she inhabits.
  Naturally, a purely thematic study of Argentine
expressionism is possible. The characters and narrators
of expressionist writings openly despair of finding objectively verifiable truths, of discerning a pattern in the
events that befall them or of learning the rules that
govern the universe. Their words express truths that are
irrational, visionary, chaotic and antiscientific. However, expressionistic statements, outcries and denuncia-
tions are not the only manifestation of expressionism in
the writings. This study does consider the strongly
expressionistic sentiments voiced by the characters and
narrators. It sees these statements as reinforced and
reiterated by such structural devices as the absence of
a trustworthy narrative voice, the omission of important
data about the characters, chaotic construction and an
allover attempt to prevent the reader from obtaining a
clear picture of what transpires in the plot. As a con-
sequence, this study will not only identify the antirationalist, antirealist thematic statements of expressionism, but also point out some structural devices that
lend support to these assertions. We hope in this way
to describe many aspects of expressionism and to draw
attention to more of its fundamental features.

V

  The reader of a study on any literary "ism" is
entitled to know from the outset whether that study will
seek manifestations of, say, expressionism in literature
of all periods or only in that of a designated period.
This decision is so important in the study of a literary
movement that it is often called "the problem of the isms."
This study will impose a time limit, roughly 1915-40, on
occurrences of expressionism. For the following reasons,
it seems appropriate.
  René Wellek in his famous essay "The Concept of the
Baroque" argues against denominating certain features as
baroque and all literature that exhibits these features

as baroque literature. His reasons are applicable to the
study of all "isms." Wellek describes the vogue of the
critical classification baroque, a vogue which led to the
misapplication and misappropriation of the term. Using
examples that will horrify or amuse the reader, Wellek
describes efforts to classify as baroque the most unlikely
and disparate writings. These absurdities are partly the
work of critics more eager to champion a cause than to
explore a critical concept.[52] However, Wellek finds
responsible commentators also straying far afield in their
application of the term. He attributes such difficulties
to excessive reliance on a particular set of identifying
features as an absolute measure of baroque. "One must
acknowledge that all stylistic devices may occur at almost
all times,"[53] he concludes. Nor will he place much hope
in definitions based on ideological, sociological, psychological or national characteristics.

Despite his rejection of these definitions of the
baroque, Wellek believes that there really was such a movement and that it left mankind with recognizably baroque
writings. "Baroque obviously arose in the most diverse
countries, almost simultaneously, in reaction against
preceding forms,"[54] he asserts, and he might well have
said the same for expressionism. Convinced that there
definitely was a "style which came after the Renaissance
but preceded actual neoclassicism,"[55] Wellek urges critics
to recognize this style as something that exists independ-
ently of their attempts to characterize it. The problem
for critical discussion, then, is to formulate a general
characterization that will apply to this pre-existing
baroque movement, not to create a new category and seek
examples that will fit into it.

Wellek recommends that critics examine the work of
this period of literary history to discover its most salient formal characteristics and the ideas it typically
reflects. Using both formal and ideological criteria,
critics may work toward an accurate description of a
literary phenomenon that can already be recognized by a
learned and perceptive reader. To introduce into the
discussion writings from other periods that exhibit one
or more of the features of the movement under scrutiny
is merely to make a difficult task more confusing.

So it is with this discussion of expressionism. To
move toward a description or characterization of expressionism as it appeared in Argentine literature of 1915-40
is its aim. The discussion of expressionistic characteristics of works dating before or after that period is quite
another matter, mainly outside the scope of the present
study. This is particularly important if one considers
the points of congruence between expressionism and the
nueva narrativa of the fifties, sixties and seventies in
Latin America. If this study were to include works up to
the present time, it would quickly grow to unmanageable
proportions.

Instead, let us consider the writers of the nueva
narrativa to be the spiritual heirs of the expressionists.
Then the legacy of expressionism can be seen in the later
works: the attempt to bypass the rational, the rejection
of the aims of realism, the idea that a literary work is
a figurative, distorted, mythified representation of real-

ity and not a direct transcription. The writers of works of "magical realism" may have conformed very nearly to the main tenets of expressionism, but they are to be considered the descendants of the expressionists, not expressionists *strictu sensu*. Indeed, it is already a commonplace of Latin American literary history to refer to Borges, Macedonio Fernández or Arlt as a precursor or ancestor of the *nueva narrativa*. This study is concerned with those ancestors, but what is true of the ancestors may be equally true of their descendants.

There is a second reason for imposing a time focus besides the pragmatic one of limiting the scope of the discussion. René Wellek believes that the baroque really existed all along, even though "the very existence of such a style has been obscured by the extension given to the term Elizabethan and by the narrow limits of the one competing traditional term: 'metaphysical'."[56] That is, something occurred in literary history independent of the term or terms that critics apply to it. Similarly, we believe something happened in Argentine literature in the twenties and thirties that affected both certain "elitist" and certain "proletarian" writers, driving them away from linear, well-developed plots with verisimilar characters and toward fragmented, disorienting fictions that reflected reality in a highly metaphorical fashion. The same massive fragmentation appears in the same period in the works of several authors. Thus, even if it were shown to be unlike the fragmentation that characterized German expressionist literature, it would still exist as a notable feature of some Argentine literary movement. If this Latin American movement were shown to be fundamentally unlike German expressionism, it could still be characterized and described as an independent phenomenon. Naturally, the Argentine "ism" could no longer justifiably be called expressionism, but its study under another name would still be possible and desirable.

Thus the use of a time focus also reflects the fact that the works herein studied all came out of an "ism" or period movement. Something happened to Latin American literature during the years between the wars, producing changes whose effects can still be perceived in contemporary works. This moment of change can be seen in the works produced during the key years of this innovation, where they first appeared. The works that concern this study are the works of the men who altered the course of Latin American fiction.

The task of this study, then, is not to formulate a list of necessary and sufficient features for the definition and identification of international expressionism. Rather, it starts with a number of innovative, disconcerting works representative of Latin American expressionism. The problem is to characterize the nature of the innovation that these works represent and to show that it is another manifestation of the great twentieth-century esthetic upheaval that produced German expressionism. Far from offering a new, absolute definition for expressionism, we will try to conform to the most accepted notions of what constitutes German expressionism, while discussing the parallel Argentine phenomenon. This generally-accepted characterization of expressionism is incomplete and pro-

visional: essentially, the general recognition of certain
features of literary work as typically expressionistic.
Literary criticism may someday arrive at an understanding
of some basic underlying axes determining the various
"isms," but that is a very different sort of critical task.
The present study does not attempt to improve or refine
existing characterizations of expressionism, but merely to
demonstrate their applicability to Argentina's *entreguerre*
outbreak of literary renovation. If they can be applied,
it is because expressionism, like the baroque, "arose in
the most diverse countries, almost simultaneously, in reaction against preceding art forms."[57] It answered the need
for a form of literary expression appropriate to twentieth-
century anxieties, doubts and preoccupations.

ENDNOTES

1. Roberto Arlt, introduction to his *Los lanzallamas* (Buenos Aires: Fabril, 1968), p. 12.

2. Juan Carlos Onetti, "Semblanza de un genio rioplatense," in *Nueva novela latinoamericana*, ed. Jorge Lafforgue (Buenos Aires: Paidós, 1969-72), II, 374.

3. Jean Franco, *The Modern Culture of Latin America* (Middlesex, England: Penguin, 1970), p. 285.

4. Arlt, *Los lanzallamas*, pp. 11-12.

5. Adolfo Prieto, "La fantasía y lo fantástico en la obra de Roberto Arlt," in Roberto Arlt, *Un relato inédito de Roberto Arlt* (Buenos Aires: Tiempo Contemporáneo, 1968), p. 10.

6. Prieto, p. 11.

7. Noé Jitrik, "Bipolaridad en la historia de la literatura argentina," in his *Ensayos y estudios de literatura argentina* (Buenos Aires: Galerna, 1970), p. 236.

8. Jitrik, p. 248.

9. David Viñas, introduction to Armando Discépolo, *Obras escogidas*, ed. David Viñas (Buenos Aires: Jorge Alvarez, 1969), I, vii-lxvi.

10. Viñas, "El escritor vacilante: Arlt, Boedo y Discépolo," in his *Literatura argentina y realidad política, de Sarmiento a Cortázar* (Buenos Aires: Siglo Veinte, 1971), pp. 67-73.

11. Guillermo de Torre, "Para la prehistoria ultraísta de Borges," *Hispania*, 47 (1964), 457-63. Also in *Cuadernos hispanoamericanos*, No. 169 (1964), 5-15.

12. Jorge Luis Borges, "El Golem," in his *Obras completas* (Buenos Aires: Emecé, 1974), p. 885.

13. Borges, p. 710.

14. Rodolfo Cardona, *Ramón: A Study of Ramón Gómez de la Serna and His Works* (New York: Eliseo Torres and Sons, 1957), p. 9.

15. Rita Mazzetti Gardiol, *Ramón Gómez de la Serna* (New York: Twayne Publishers, 1974), pp. 21-28.

16. Victoria Ocampo, *Diálogo con Borges* (Buenos Aires: Sur, 1969), p. 75.

17. Alicia Borinsky, "Correspondencia de Macedonio Fernández a Gómez de la Serna," *Revista iberoamericana*, 36 (1970), 101-23.

18. Arlt, *Aguafuertes porteñas* (Buenos Aires: Losada, 1958), p. 78.

19. Prieto, pp. 19-20.

20. René Wellek, "The Concept of Baroque," in his *Concepts of Criticism* (New Haven: Yale, 1964), p. 88.

21. Arlt, *Aguafuertes españolas* (Buenos Aires: Talleres Gráficos Argentinos L.J. Rosso, 1936).

22. Borges, cited in Jorge Lafforgue, "La narrativa argentina actual," in *Nueva novela latinoamericana,* I, p. 17.

23. Borinsky, pp. 101-04.

24. Prieto, p. 20.

25. Arlt, *Aguafuertes porteñas,* p. 78.

26. Arlt, *Aguafuertes porteñas,* p. 160.

27. Arlt, *Aguafuertes porteñas,* p. 78.

28. Jitrik, pp. 229-37.

29. Viñas, introduction to Discépolo, pp. xix-xx.

30. Siegfried Kracauer, *From Caligari to Hitler, a Psychological History of the German Film* (Princeton, N.J.:   Princeton, 1966).

31. Walter H. Sokel, *The Writer in Extremis: Expressionism in Twentieth-Century Literature* (Stanford: Stanford University Press, 1959).

32. Richard Samuel, and R. Hinton Thomas, *Expressionism in German Life, Literature and the Theatre* (Philadelphia: Albert Saifer, 1971).

33. Henry Hatfield, *Modern German Literature* (New York: St. Martin's Press, 1967), pp. 60-61.

34. Viñas, introduction to Discépolo, pp. vii-lxvi.   Mirta Arlt makes a similar point about Arlt's internationality in her introduction to Arlt, *Los lanzallamas,* pp. 7-10.

35. Mirta Arlt, cited by Eduardo González Lanuza, *Roberto Arlt* (Buenos Aires: Centro Editor, 1971), p. 43.

36. Kasimir Edschmid, cited by Hatfield, p. 58.

37. Kurt Pinthus, cited by Hatfield, p. 60.

38. Edschmid, cited by Sokel, p. 32.

39. David William Foster, *Unamuno and the Novel as Expressionistic Conceit* (Hato Rey, P.R.: Inter American University Press, 1973), p. 7.

40. Victor Lange, *Modern German Literature* (Port Washington, N.Y.: Kennikat Press, 1967), pp. 79-91.

41. Samuel and Thomas, p. 26.

42. Derek van Abbé, *Image of a People* (New York: Barnes and Noble, 1964), p. 137.

43. Wolfgang Kayser, *Interpretación y análisis de la obra literaria*, 4. ed. rev. (Madrid: Gredos, 1961), p. 230.

44. Kayser, p. 193.

45. See Eduardo González Lanuza, *Roberto Arlt* (Buenos Aires: Centro Editor de America Latina, 1971), on chaotic structure in Arlt as a legitimate literary recourse rather than a result of negligence, pp. 82-83. González Lanuza also justifies Arlt's aberrant linguistic expression as a literarily-based deviation with the exception of the journalistic notes, which he sees as reflecting hasty composition, pp. 27-31.

46. Arlt, *El criador de gorilas* (Buenos Aires: Editorial Universitaria, 1964), dedication page.

47. Arlt, introduction to *Los lanzallamas*, pp. 11-12.

48. Jitrik, p. 248.

49. Onetti, p. 374.

50. Discépolo, *Entre el hierro*, in his *Obras escogidas*, p. 25.

51. Discépolo, p. 8.

52. Wellek, pp. 94-95.

53. Wellek, p. 102.

54. Wellek, p. 105.

55. Wellek, p. 113.

56. Wellek, p. 113.

57. Wellek, p. 105.

Chapter 2

The Loss of Faith in Reason

Expressionism, as a movement, called into question the usefulness of human reason in understanding man. Literary works began to suggest that human existence was by its very nature unamenable to rational analysis. No longer was it tenable to maintain, as does an exemplary fool in a Discépolo play, that "Todo se consigue con lógica y con voluntad."[1] Instead, it seemed that the things that could be ascertained or governed by logical effort were not even central to man's existence.

German expressionists doubted what reason could accomplish and tried, through their works, to awaken the same doubts in the reader or playgoer. They embraced the work of philosophers who voiced a similar skepticism. One commonly finds historians of German expressionism linking that movement's wariness of ratiocination with the general acceptance of the same ideas in philosophical treatises. For instance, one history states: "In 1907 the appearance of Bergson's *L'Evolution Créatrice,* which was widely read in Germany, gave this conception and added stimulus. Bergson sought to demonstrate the helplessness of analytical reasoning in the face of the deeper problems of existence. In place of mathematical investigation he preached the need for intuition which 'is that type of intellectual assimilation by means of which one penetrates into the inner essence of an object.' Moreover, as Bergson interpreted it, intuition revealed a fact dear to the hearts of the Expressionists, that the nature of the world lay in movement, to which he applied the term 'creative development.'"[2] Parallels have also been found between the expressionists' questioning of rationality and the same doubts voiced by other philosophers, by essayists and by orators or politicians. Impatience with rational discourse and analytical thought, with waiting for the "progress" promised by science and technology, became a prominent feature of the intellectual climate.[3]

Nowhere was this disillusionment with science and reason more unmistakably expressed than in literature. Authors resorted to the most extreme means to prevent their reader from approaching the characters and situations of a literary work in an analytical spirit. Wolfgang Kayser describes the expressionists as having recourse to "La negligencia frente a la unidad de acción y la ausencia de una estructuración rígida"[4] in the theater and, at the linguistic level, "una rotura de todos los vínculos lingüísticos y ...un balbuceo que ya no era lengua."[5] Walter H. Sokel characterizes the expressionist as a man continually and publicly confronting "the dark chaos of life."[6] According to Sokel, the expressionist felt that since "the truth of the world was horror and meaningless-

ness,"[7] he must disregard all rules and conventional constraints in his efforts to wrest some intuitive, irrational meaning out of that chaos. Another commentator posits
Dada as expressionism's first flowering because, "convinced the contemporary world was a madhouse, the Dadaists
aimed to convey a sense of the paradoxical, grotesque and
absurd."[8]

The search for alternatives to rational perception
and representation of experience has been one of the most
lasting innovations to come out of the ferment of the early
twentieth century. The idea of using literature to circumvent the rational, the scientific and the civilized is a
concept central to the *nueva narrativa* of the fifties,
sixties and seventies. Both critics and writers of these
latter-day irrationalist works have been quick to recognize
them as descendants of the great vanguardistic movements
of the *entreguerre* period. Ernesto Sábato (b.1911) has been
perhaps the most eager to acknowledge the importance of
this antirationalistic literature in providing him with a
fresh way of perceiving reality after the scientific model
had proved inadequate. Sábato's disillusionment with
science, abandonment of a promising career as atomic
researcher and subsequent reorganization of his outlook
by giving prominence to the irrational and intuitive all
are well-known.[9] So is Sábato's continued belief in literature as a remedy for hyperrationalism, "una salida que
me permitiera acceder al hombre concreto enajenado por
una civilización tecnolátrica."[10] Throughout his writings,
Sábato has testified to the importance of literature as a
liberation from dependency on reason and science: "¡Cómo
comprendí entonces el valor moral del surrealismo, su
fuerza destructiva contra los mitos de una civilización
terminada, su fuego purificador...."[11]

Of all the manifestations of the scientific quest to
explain, predict and remedy the world, none was more odious
to the expressionist than the investigations of social
scientists. "The Expressionist...hates all work based on
what he regards as the misleading factor of psychology
and despises literature dealing with such trifles as social
success or failure."[12] states one history of the movement.
The expressionists looked on the social sciences as an
encroachment on what had been the province of the humani-
ties: the contemplation of human beings. The flourishing
social sciences seemed bent on reducing the mysterious
complexities of human conduct and feelings to little more
than rule-governed behavior. Social scientists, moreover,
began their study of man with data based on observable
phenomena. One of the main tenets of expressionism was
the spurning of observable realities. Kasimir Edschmid,
for example, exhorted man to remain unsatisfied with what
he could observe from without, for the observable aspect
was always a distortion. He held that no phenomenon would
yield up its meaning "until its true form has been recognized, until it is liberated from the muffled restraint
of a false reality, until everything that is latent within
it is expressed."[13]

The social sciences, which claimed to study man from
without on the basis of scientific principles, alarmed the

expressionists particularly. Expressionism considered the most significant aspects of man to be inaccessible to purely analytical investigation. Julio Cortázar describes the literary innovations of this century as refutations of "that false realism that consists of believing that all things can be described and explained...as part of a world ruled more or less harmoniously by a system of law of principles, of cause and effect relationships or defined psychologies, of well-mapped geographies." Avoiding such arrogant assumptions, twentieth-century literature suggests the governance of the universe is "more secret, and less communicable,"[14] and hence cannot be grasped by logic alone.

Expressionism sought to convince the reader of the severe limitations of reason, both as a means of comprehending and as panacea. Logical procedures seemed inefficacious when applied to the essentially irrational existence of human beings. Literature since the great innovative "isms" of the early twentieth century "sostiene que los hombres, en la ficcion como en la realidad, no obedecen a las leyes de la lógica," in the words of Ernesto Sábato.[15]

II

How does expressionism seek to wean man from his fatuous dependence on reason? It would be a poor generalization to say that literature is opposed to reason. Literature may, in fact, employ reasonable arguments as part of its strategy to show that logic has its limits. The reader may be obliged to rethink his presuppositions and expectations concerning rationality. As Sabato says, "Es el mismo pensamiento que nos ha vuelto cautos, al revelarnos sus propios límites en esta quiebra general de nuestra época."[16] What is being argued is the inapplicability of reason to certain areas of human existence. For example, an Arlt character known as the Astrologer inveighs against the notion that political campaigns can successfully appeal to reason. He argues, reasonably enough, that men crave satisfactions from their participation in political life that are irrational ones. Therefore it would be self-defeating for a political organization to make reasoned appeals to the public. Rather, such a group should offer fulfillment of spiritual needs and yearnings: "le serviremos la felicidad bien cocinada y la humanidad engullirá gozosamente la divina bazofia."[17]

When the Astrologer argues his political beliefs, statements that are essentially true for the Arltian universe are put forth. The reader is brought toward an expressionist's antirationalistic view of politics because that view is presented to him in a more or less reasonable manner. On the other hand, the Astrologer has many rhetorical ploys which bypass rational discourse altogether. He invites actors playing fictitious roles to political planning meetings, stages a mock execution, draws up astrological charts and plays the most varied roles to suit his needs of the moment. Like the Astrologer, the expressionistic novel sometimes argues against placing too much faith in ratiocination and at other times bewilders the reader with irrational stratagems that prevent him from approaching the work in too rational and linear a fashion.

Of the arguments against the cult of reason, perhaps the most common is the fictional presentation of confused human situations that refuse to respond to the application of reason. Rationalistic characters, however clever and quick-thinking they may be, prove miserable failures in their attempts to ameliorate human difficulties. Other characters, though, voice doubts about the applicability of reason to such subjective matters. Their skepticism may win adherents as the logical procedures fail to produce the desired improvement. The audience comes to see the characters who trust too much in reason as exemplary fools.

Two expressionist plays that show reason failing to bring order to tangled human affairs are Roberto Arlt's *El desierto entra a la ciudad* (1952) and Armando Discépolo's *Entre el hierro* (1910). In the posthumous Arlt work, the characters struggle to deal rationally with their common plight, only to fail miserably. Not only is no valid solution proposed during a lengthy attempt at rational discourse, but the participants end up more confused, unhappy and at odds with the universe. In Discépolo's play, on the other hand, the characters do no harm with their logical comments on their problems. Rather, the disconcerting element is the lack of connection between the formulation of insightful, apt and logical comments on one's situation and the ability to take sensible action to improve that situation. In each case, human beings are shown as inherently irrational creatures. Reason appears quite useless against the dark forces that actually determine what people feel and how they behave.

Arlt's *El desierto entra a la ciudad* is our instance of a play so thoroughgoing in its demythification of reason that it presents reason as not only no remedy for the bedeviled, but in fact as something that makes a confused situation worse. The first act of the play sets up a situation of great stress for a community modeled along the lines of Roman government circles, but situated in 1942. The incessant merrymaking necessary to the functioning of the gathering has begun to cloy on its Caesar, and he has been manifesting deep discontent. His hangers-on cannot accept Caesar's rejection of their high-living days, because if they are terminated the merrymakers will be disbanded and sent back to the oppressive jobs they previously held in the city. Indeed, one may see the expressionistic depiction of the world as madhouse not only in the mindless cavorting about the pseudo-Romans are willing to accept in return for residence in the community, but in the implied worse horror of forming part of the bureaucratic machinery needed to run a twentieth-century society. Working life is so bad that the merrymakers would tolerate the most stressful situation with Caesar rather than go back. "En las oficinas se burlarán de nuestra vuelta," one pleads, while another claims "Ya nunca más podremos llevar la contabilidad con inocencia."[18] Another, unnerved by the threat to his way of life, forgets his adulatory stance and snarls at Caesar: "¡Bucólico estás!" (p. 177).

The second act of the play is the one that serves to demythify logic. The pseudo-Romans have formed a tribunal to deal with the intolerably stressful situation in a logical, structured fashion. At first the attempt appears likely to succeed. While in the first act the neo-Romans are in panic over Caesar's behavior, at the outset of the second they calmly prepare to debate one aspect of the matter, whether Caesar has lost his wits. A first case is made for the man's evident madness based on the testimony of a witness. However, this logical procedure does not resolve the matter or even shed light on it. The testimony merely brings forth fresh confusion. A priest reinterprets the alleged manifestations of madness as the signs of burgeoning saintliness and spiritual awakening. The difficulty seems to be that the same actions may be taken as indicative of different underlying states, as suits the observer or listener. As a cynical lame man remarks, Caesar's intention is manifestly noble "si viene de un cuerdo" (p. 188). The tribunal is unwilling to abandon the procedure of hearing testimony, and plead for some less ambiguous manifestation of Caesar's supposed insanity: "¿No dice incoherencias?" (p. 189).

A secondary complication is the lack of common criteria for distinguishing madness from sanity. The priest worries lest "se califique de insano a un hombre tocado por la gracia de Dios. Con este criterio, todos los santos...debieron ser internados en un manicomio" (p. 190). A lawyer points out that saintliness and madness today cannot be held to standards established in the days of the great saints. The multiplicity of complicating factors grows unwieldy when two financial backers appear. To them, Caesar is sane providing that "los negocios marchen con la regularidad que es indispensable al pago de los dividendos, intereses y amortizaciones" (p. 192). The cynical lame man doubts objectivity obtains when all concerned must either follow Caesar on his ascetic retreat or return to dehumanizing city life. The ambiguities and contradictions that constitute human existence are what preclude assessing Caesar's sanity.

The neo-Romans will not yet despair of applying logic to life. They attempt to set up an experiment which can be observed by everyone rather than rely on testimony from a witness. The test will consist of planting a cadaver, or failing that, a corpselike dummy, which Caesar, if he is mad, will try to bring back to life. It is unable to surmount the problems inherent in defining sanity and madness. Someone objects that Caesar might be mad enough to attempt to revive a corpse, but not the dummy that the neo-Romans plan to use in the test. Another objects that Caesar's madness may not manifest itself in the attempt to work miracles. A woman convinced of Caesar's wonder-working power offers to kill herself and be revived by the leader. The simple test situation turns out to be so dizzyingly fraught with complications that the neo-Romans fear for their sanity. "En esta casa se han vuelto locos todos," says one, while another compares the neo-Romans, joined in rational discourse, to "la antesala de un manicomio" (p. 196). The discussants' willingness to hear the advice of an astrologer is the definitive sign of their despair of finding an answer through reasoned interchange of ideas. The astrologer's discourse does not pretend to be logical. His is the rhetoric of soothing nonsense, but it captures the attention and lifts the spirits of the neo-Romans. He is the only speaker able to hold the floor without being interrupted by some outraged member of the audience. Under his spell, the neo-Romans calm down and are soon chattily admitting to one another that they have always been tempted to consult an astrologer. Relaxation is only possible when the rigors of rationality are jettisoned.

The comment that the whole of the second act presents is that the application of rational discourse to human problems is severely limited by the chaotic nature of the world. The characters strive to set up rational criteria for determining madness, but the ambiguous nature of human behavior and the diversity of interests impeding objective assessment are too overwhelming. If the world is such a madhouse, the characters are just as well off listening to the soothing nonsense of an astrologer as attempting a rational assault on the disordered expressionistic world.

III

While in Arlt the effort to apply reason to real-life problems causes compounded difficulties, in Discépolo's *Entre el hierro* the failure of reason manifests itself in a disassociation between the characters' often reasonable commentary on their situations and their irrational behavior. The irrational nature of existence is made even more evident by the often excellent logic of what the characters say, since one expects them to make an application of these well-considered insights in the field of action. Instead, something in the illogical universe posited by the expressionists prevents the ability to describe oneself rationally from becoming an ability to act in a way that will not be self-destructive.

Only two decisive events occur during *Entre el hierro*. One, the marriage of a clever young woman to a dim-witted lout, occurs during the time gap between the first and second acts, but is anticipated during the first act. The other, her killing of the loutish husband during one of the quarrels that punctuate the work, ends the play. Most of the action, then, is behavior in everyday situations, but behavior so clearly opposed to the best interests of the characters as to be grotesque. The heroine repeatedly fails to assert herself or to take decisive action. She backs down in confrontations with her husband, letting him so subjugate her that he can object to her habit of dreaming while asleep. In a rupture with good sense, she fails to dismiss a listless suitor even when he provokes the malicious gossip of neighbors and the jealousy of the hot-tempered husband. Her passivity is exaggerated to an expressionistic extent. She calls herself "la muerta" (p. 4), while another character comments that he soon expects to find her "hecha mármol contra la mesa" (p. 4). The abulic condition of her suitor is just as hyper-

bolic in its manifestations. Although his courtship pro-
ceeds at considerable risk, it could hardly be called
impetuous: "Adela...discúlpeme.... Haciendo un esfuerzo
de coloso he conseguido pasar del patio al otro cuarto.
Para eso he necesitado desplegar una energía desconocida
en mí" (p. 47). David Viñas found the most expressionistic feature of this work to be the grotesquely hyperbolic
degeneration that overtakes the characters. [19]
     Viñas found it noteworthy that this expressionistic
deterioration should occur in the context of a *sainete,*
usually a light, sentimental drama. He called this rupture
a "refinamiento del sainete tradicional (o del naturalismo
discursivo) en tránsito al grotesco." [20] A yet more startling
deviation from the expected is the lucid comments and self-
appraisals made by characters who cannot apply reason to
the governance of their lives. They cannot correct the
disordered way in which they conduct their affairs, but
only recognize it and verbalize about it. For instance,
in the first act Adela's friends point out the unwisdom
of her engagement to a stupid, surly man. The reader must
concur, for the fiance appears on stage and gives every
evidence of being dim-witted and obsessively jealous.
     Unwilling to consider the evident irrationalism of the
marriage, the bride evades any attempt to engage her in
rational discourse concerning her upcoming marriage. Concerned friends cannot elicit from her any valid reason why
she should marry such an unworthy man. One of them says
bluntly: "Oh, quién razona con vos esta noche. Lo que
tiene León es un carácter un tanto brusco y sobre todo unos
celos indomables. Oílo. Sos desmasiado linda, y lo que
es peor, demasiado inteligente para él. Debías haberlo
comprendido ya, aviniéndote a sus fallas. ¿Cuál es el
mérito de los mejores, entonces?" (p. 8). Accused not
only of conducting her own life unwisely but also of insulting the notion that the world has some logic to it,
the heroine is vague and cryptic, answering only "Apartarse"
(p. 8). She rejects the idea that she ought to bring more
logic to bear on her life situation, saying "lo que me
sobra es el frío de la comprensión" (p. 7). This statement is close to the expressionistic tenet that the world
is not a place receptive or responsive to reasoning.
Adela is unwilling to hear sensible objectives to her
planned marriage, and denies that a reasoned discussion
can make life itself more reasonable. "No hablemos más
del asunto," she pleads, "no arribaríamos a nada razonable"
(p. 24). Reproached with excessive silence and withdrawal,
she disparages the verbal communication by which other
characters reason with one another and themselves: "Bah
¿y qué voy a decir que no haya dicho antes?" (p. 5).
     The other characters are not so willing to accept this
view of the world as a place so arbitrary as not to be
worth reasoning about. They invent possible reasons for
the marriage, imagining the bride to be a martyr possessed
by an exaggerated sense of duty, "sumisa" (p. 29) and
"soportadora" by nature (p. 24). One explains that the
girl's mother had bound the ill-matched couple from her
deathbed, but another objects that deathbed promises have
no binding value. These explanations do not fit well with

the heroine's opinions about love and duty when she is
speaking of abstract values rather than of her own case.
She says "No, la familia es amor puramente, porque el
hombre nace libre y el deber es una cadena insoportable
si no se llama satisfacción" (p. 7), pointing out that
the family structure common in her environment effectively
blocks women from enjoying either love or a sense of fulfillment through duties accomplished. In fact, she
carries on a lively debate with an older character who
champions the primacy of duty. Thus it would appear that
she has no objection to reasoning as such, and can engage
in it herself, but finds it self-defeating to try to apply
reasoning to the practical matters of this absurd world.
   The events of the play invalidate yet another suggested reason for the heroine's behavior, that is, that she
is frightened of her husband's latent brutality. In the
final quarrel she nearly provokes her husband into killing
the listless suitor, rescues the suitor at the last minute
and kills the husband. In short, she demonstrates that
she holds the whip psychologically. Indeed, her husband
might better have been frightened of her latent brutality.
None of the explanations formulated by her friends really
explains her behavior in an adequate or insightful way;
the "reasons" are attempts not to see the world as the
chaos that Adela and, indeed, one of the main tenets of
expressionism hold it to be.
   Adela's renunciation of logic as a mechanism for
governing one's life is seconded by two characters who
destroy themselves with alcohol without ever losing their
ability to summarize their own life situations. One quite
correctly sums up his shortcomings as a guest: "Yo ya no
sirvo sino para entibiar la alegría" (p. 60). He points
out that a less sodden companion "Está aburrido de aguan-
tarme" (p. 58). Reproached with inadequate raising of
his children, he agrees at once: "Hay que tener mucha
voluntad y ningún vicio para crear...¡que se arreglen! yo
no tengo" (p. 59). At one point he even propounds a
societal explanation for his drinking: "¿Por qué chupo?...
El *fierro* para levantar casas de ricos precisa alcohol
para amasarse...y la costumbre domina. ¿Es feo, eh? Es
feo estar así, pero domina" (pp. 58-59). Neither the
other characters nor the reader could quarrel with the
veracity of these commentaries. However, no application
is made of these insights to the practical matter of how
not to be destroyed by life.
   In both the Arlt and Discépolo plays, characters
elaborate a number of insightful and rational statements.
However, the disorder of the world is too thoroughgoing
to be resolved with an application of clear thinking. The
characters may be most eager to believe that life is not
altogether absurd and grotesque, insisting, as does a
Discépolo character, that "Todo se consigue con lógica y
con voluntad" (p. 25). The expressionistic world confusion
that besets the characters proves him altogether wrong.
In Arlt's play, all of the second act up to the appearance
of the Astrologer is given over to an earnest attempt by
the characters to remedy a deteriorating situation by discussing it rationally and determining the best course of
action.

Other characters doubt that one can take arms against
the world's illogic with ordered thinking. A Discépolo
character comments paradoxically but accurately on his
fellows: "La razón no les sirve sino para hacerse irracionales" (p. 42). The heroine interrupts another character's rationalizing remarks, saying: "¡Oh cuántas
palabras para no querer, huecas de sentido, no las comprendo,
no quiero comprenderlas!" (p. 7). In turn, a would-be
counselor complains that Adela makes use of rational discourse to "agarrar todo del lado oscuro y feo" and that,
rather than penetrating a subject through ratiocination,
she is merely engaging in sterile brooding (p. 6). He
suggests it is counterproductive to analyze life: "Hum...
estás filósofa y...mirá, los filósofos son como los racimos
de uva...Tené éste...¡Ja!...mucho grano, muy maduro, pero
si lo dejás colgado del parral se pudre" (p. 6). Rather
than reason about life phenomena, he urges her to experience
them without the interference of her rational faculties.

Thus Discépolo's play insults our belief that someone
who is insightful about human problems, particularly his
own, is better prepared to deal with existence. The characters in *Entre el hierro* are articulate and often eloquent
about the difficulties that they face. Indeed, they often
engage in thoughtful debate on such subjects as love, duty
and human debilities. Yet they persist in irrationally
destroying themselves and one another.
Jorge Luis Borges's 1935 *Historia universal de la
infamia* constitutes another kind of mockery of the human
mania to apply reason to all phenomena. In the case of
the *Historia universal*, it is not the characters who are
eager to think clearly about life. Rather, the reader's
potential for seeing logical interrelationships and meaningful patterns in the material he reads is capriciously
frustrated. The instrument of this frustration is a narrator who, while initially appearing to present a coherent
and significant body of information, really claims the
reader's attention in order to bombard it with isolated
and ultimately meaningless data. He does not attempt to
make logical sense of the "dark chaos of life"[21] as posited
by expressionism, concurring that "the world was a madhouse."[22] Moreover, he ridicules the reader's desires
for coherence and meaning by taking measures that will
awaken such expectations, only to disappoint them.
The first of these measures is the subject matter of
the work: the destructive behavior of individuals who
would once have been classified as "morally insane" and
today are "sociopaths." Surely there is no area in which
man would more like to apply rational inquiry and remedial
measures than in the control of violent behavior. The erad-
ication of human violence has long been a dream of Utopians,
poets, seers and the more optimistic representatives of the
various social sciences. Even if we cannot suppress man's
potential for wreaking havoc, we would dearly love to
understand it, to predict it and hence to control it. As
witness to this desire to comprehend, one has only to consider the impact of such works as Hannah Arendt's *Eichmann
in Jerusalem: a Report on the Banality of Evil*[23] and Konrad

Lorenz's *On Aggression*.[24]   In literature, the need to make
some sense out of the events of the Third Reich has gener-
ated a vast body of work. The literary work may offer an
original treatment or a well-accepted discussion of the
problem of human evil. However, the reader does demand
that the work actually confront the problem rather than
dismiss it in a frivolous fashion, as something devoid of
significance or transcendence. Even the most eccentric,
outrageous explanation is better than none at all.
      Yet, this refusal to explain or to draw any meaningful
generalization is all *Historia universal* offers. The work
betrays the very enterprise on which it embarks: the investigation of evil. Capriciously, it mimics the code of such
genuinely explanatory works as criminology textbooks or
popularizations of sociological research. The narrative
voice of the *Historia* is an authoritative-sounding one,
with all the trappings of a serious student of human
behavior. Borges makes use of documentation, literary and
general-culture references and facts from related disciplines. Above all he relies on the presentation of case
histories, a standard device for the study and discussion
of deviant behavior. These cases ought, if the rationalist
social-science model is followed, to lead narrator and
reader toward a general characterization of infamy. The
presupposition is that there are rules that govern infamy
and that such rules can be discovered by a rational procedure: the study of typical occurrences. The code reassures the reader that he is not being subjected to so much
gratuitously assembled data, but rather that it will all
eventually prove to have meaning. More importantly, it
reinforces the idea that social phenomena can be discussed
in a principled, scientific way with fruitful results.
Borges uses the code but disrupts it, thus depriving the
reader of the orderly conclusion he has been led to expect.
Thus he also casts doubt on the larger question: is man's
reason capable of discovering the patterns underlying his
behaviors?

V

      One of the most bewildering habits of this unillu-
minating narrator is his mania for gathering all manner of
data supposedly relevant to the discussion but ultimately
without bearing on the matter. For instance, in "El
espantoso redentor Lazarus Morell," the reader is plunged
into a sea of information from the outset. The data-crazed
narrator begins with what he reassures us is "la causa
remota" of this particular outbreak of infamy, the introduction of slaves into the New World, where some other,
distant slaves will eventually be swindled by Lazarus
Morell.[25]   Although the historical circumstance is prof-
fered as explanation, it not only fails to shed light on
the actions of Morell, but bears witness to the frailty of
human powers of reasoning: "En 1517 el P. Bartolomé de
las Casas tuvo mucha lástima de los indios que se extenua-
ban en los laboriosos infiernos de las minas de oro antillanas y propuso la importación de negros que se extenuaran
en los laboriosos infiernos de oro antillanas" (p. 17).
As if eager to bring in evidence from all disciplines, the

narrator goes on to inform us about the Mississippi River,
the inhabitants of its drainage basin and the social structure of the antebellum South, in which Morell figures as
"canalla blanca" (p. 21). The reader is overwhelmed by a
bizarre *accumulatio* of data that, it eventually turns out,
does not allow him to account for the deviance and evil of
the infamous Morell. The narrator does not acknowledge
this deficiency in his account, but continues his barrage
of carefully-documented facts as if he had, in fact, something to contribute to an understanding of such behavior.

The chapter on a female pirate also gives out great
amounts of information, but not what one would most like
to have: information bearing on the heroine's rupture
with sexual roles and assumption of an aggressively male
mode of life. The narrator comments on this point only by
listing other occurrences of female-led piracy and attrib-
uting his heroine's break with sex stereotyping in this
most inadequate fashion: "La viuda, transfigurada por la
doble traición, congregó a los piratas" (p. 43). The
widow's outrage over the circumstances of her husband's
death is simply not sufficient to account for her anomalous
success in a man's role.

Occasionally some element of the narrator's erratic
story will suggest to the reader that an overall explanation is at hand, only to frustrate him by failing to develop
any connecting threads. For instance, on at least two
occasions the historian of evil suggests that female piracy
is an outgrowth of a severe confusion of sexual identity.
He quotes one woman pirate as declaring that "la profesión
de pirata no era para cualquiera, y que para ejercerla con
dignidad, era preciso ser un hombre de acción, como ella"
(p. 41). He describes at some length the uncommonly ugly
piratess, as though preparing to hypothesize that inability
to meet societal expectations for women led her to compete
on purely male terms. However, neither of these suggested
generalizations is ever drawn, and the historian rushes on
to the next isolated datum that, in turn, will never form
part of an integrated whole. The narrator has been drawn
to the subject of female piracy because it is so anomalous,
but makes no attempt to explain the anomaly.

Indeed, some of his information compounds one's puz-
zlement, for it emphasizes the subjugation of women in that
time and place. "La tripulación viajaba con sus mujeres,
pero el capitan con su harem, que era de cinco o seis,
y que solían renovar las victorias" (p. 46). One grows all
the more anxious to understand how, if women were spoils
or provisions, one woman could assume command. The narrator, though, does not feel impelled to interpret the welter
of information with which he assaults the reader.

While the information one would like to have is withheld, the historian supplies a good deal of nonessential
data. He describes the colors of the pirate fleet, the
prose of the piratess, life among the pirate crew and
other matters that, though curious and amusing, say
nothing about infamy or about female agression. The entire
chapter constitutes a mocking frustration of the human
mania to seek significance in all phenomena, from the ris-
ing of the moon to devastating wars. Indeed, even the
basic distinction between what is important and germane

and what is trivial and irrelevant seems to have broken
down in the general confusion.

As well as inundating the reader in unassimilable
information, the narrator foils his desire to interpret
and understand by presenting case histories chosen for
their utterly aberrant features. The most rational function of case histories is to provide a paradigmatic model
of some sociological or psychological phenomenon, and hence
they are selected with an eye to their consistency and
typical nature. The case histories here have just the
opposite function. They refuse to fit into a coherent
pattern or to lend support to even the vaguest general
characterization of infamy.

An instance of this procedure is the history of "Monk
Eastman, proveedor de iniquidades." Everything about
Monk's life violates our notion that those who commit
crimes do so because they have not had the opportunity to
be fully assimilated into a basically good society. To
make sense of the criminal's deviance, we would like to
think that poverty, cultural upheaval, lack of education
or family disintegration have prevented his enjoying the
benefits of the social order. Monk, however, comes from
an intact, if not monied, family and his father establishes
him in the economic order by purchasing a pet shop for his
son. The narrator himself must remark on Monk's failure
to meet our expectations: "Cosa extraña, ese malevo tor-
mentoso era hebreo" (p. 56), describing a childhood environment replete with tradition, continuity and family ties.
Everything suggests that Eastman, son of a Kosher restau-
rateur, ought to find the world a well-functioning, safe,
benign place inhabited by "varones de rabínicas barbas"
(p. 56) and the animals he delights in. Instead, he per-
sists in creating chaos and bloodshed all through his life-
time.

Indeed, all of Monk's life is full of elements which
defy attempts to incorporate them into any rational scheme.
Monk Eastman, far from supplying any typus of the gangland
killer, becomes a bizarre, hermetic figure, surrounded
even in death by adored and adoring animals. The narrator
describes him as leaving Sing Sing "todavía perplejo"
(p. 62) at the world around him. Monk's aberrance cannot
be considered a manifestation of any alienation from society, for upon leaving prison he immediately enlists in his
country's war effort. If he is not alienated in the societal sense, one would think he must be suffering from
alienation in the sense of personal madness. The narrator
does not pursue this second possibility, and the story cannot possibly be considered a psychological case history.
Monk seems an illustration of the notion which Borges was
later to formulate in his famous "Tlön, Uqbar, Orbis
Tertius": "Inútil responder que la realidad tambien está
ordenada. Quizá lo esté, pero de acuerdo a leyes divinas--
traduzco: a leyes inhumanas--que no acabamos nunca de
percibir."[26]

The cases presented in *Historia universal* are all
instances of a phenomenon we greatly wish to explain: the
persistence of violent, destructive behavior in a society
that is supposedly good and well-ordered. While appearing
to attack this problem using the familiar code of the

sociological presentation, Borges's narrator disrupts this
code and finally betrays its promise of a general characterization of infamy. Rather than reaching a significant
conclusion, the narrator is detroying in two ways our hope
of reaching such useful truths.

First, the historian inundates the reader in data
that pertains to the case studies discussed. The point of
all this amassing of data is, it turns out, notably absent,
leaving the reader with nothing but a hodgepodge of useless
facts. The case history promises to document some theory
that will eventually emerge, but the promise is not kept.
A second device for insulting the reader's desire to comprehend is the inclusion of anomalous information without
an attempt to explain the anomaly. We would like to have
classifications and categories for criminal behavior, typically "culturally deprived" on a societal level or "crim-
inally insane" on a psychological one. Then we can grasp
their unwillingness to abide by our basic societal rules
and move toward remedies. Borges's evildoers fail to
exhibit significant similarities in their behavior that
will permit us to situate them sociologically, psychologically or in any other logical fashion. Thus they insult
our desire to classify and order.

The expressionist's attempt to dethrone and demystify
reason here takes an ironic, mocking form. The narrator
initially appears to engage the rational faculties of his
reader in order to explore with him one aspect of human
existence. In this case, he employs the reasonable-
sounding code of the social scientist. Indeed, he seems
to hold forth the promise of the social sciences: that
the rules governing human behavior can be discovered by
rational, principled inquiry. However, the material presented is absolutely unamenable to rational analysis, full
of trivia and anomalies. The fact that one cannot stop
trying to find a meaningful pattern in this ragtag accumulation of facts bears witness to man's deep-seated desire
to comprehend. An essayist seeking to explore man's infamy
in a responsible manner would take advantage of this human
tendency to convince us of the validity of his generalizations. Borges's expressionistic narrator engages our
rationalizing habits of mind to show us how dogged and
arbitrary they are even in the face of the most unintelligible phenomena--a category that may well include the
world we inhabit.

VI

The Arlt and Discépolo plays and the Borges work
represent the expressionistic attempt to point out the
deficiencies of rational discourse and of approaching life
problems with logic. Two distinct forms of mockery occur
in these works. In the two dramatic works, characters who
believe in reason and in its applicability to real-life
situations are lampooned for their credulity. Such characters may be well-intentioned, articulate and clever, but
they are seriously mistaken about the nature of existence.
As adherents to the cult of reason, they misguidedly
attempt to be rational about such unruly phenomena as madness, sanity, saintliness, love, duty and the family. In

Arlt, the very application of reason to an unwieldy human
situation is the catalyst for a redoubled outbreak of confusion. In Discépolo, a grotesque effect comes from the
disassociation between the characters' logical comments
on their situations and their unwise, self-destructive
behavior.

In Borges, it is not the characters but the reader
whose dependence on reasoning is satirized. The narrator
seems to hold out to his reader the promise of a logically
satisfying work. He adopts the guise of a social scientist,
that is, of one who would explain human conduct on the
basis of scientific principles. Mimicking the sociolo-
gist's case-history presentation and his reassuringly academic code, the narrator disrupts the code and reneges on
his implied promise to arrive at some understanding of
human behavior.

The insistence that reason has only a limited applicability is, on the one hand, one of the features that
situates expressionism in its historical moment. Throughout Western culture there appeared manifestations of discontent with the excesses of rationalism. In particular,
the social sciences came under fire for their claims to be
able to study man from the outside on the basis of scientific principles alone. Not only creative artists but
also literary critics and other academic specialists voiced
concern, lest the aggressively rationalistic social sciences
overrun the humanistic studies, relegating sensibility,
intuition and esthetic pleasure to the status of hobbies.
It seemed as though the creations of the human spirit, once
they had been expropriated by the social sciences, might
come to seem no more than symptoms of some societal
deficiency.

Faced with this onslaught of rationalization, the
expressionists tried to alert readers to those sectors of
human experience that could not be subjected to purely
rational analysis. For instance, a history of German
expressionism states that "Expressionism was more than a
literary tendency; it had its counterpart in almost every
sphere of thought. About 1910 a new development can be
seen in all aspects of life and art. A decisive turn in
painting, music, sculpture and architecture had preceded
that in literature.... The 'Geisteswissenschaften' in
German universities turned from scientific research and
made the intuitive discovery of underlying experience
('Erlebnis') the aim of study. As a background to this
new spiritual activity must be set a changing world." [27]

Much as the revindication of the nonrational belongs
to the expressionistic period, it is also one of the
features of Argentine expressionism that most clearly
shows that movement as the precursor of the *nueva narrativa*
of the fifties, sixties and seventies. Even a cursory look
at the representative works of the "boom" years shows the
same devices used to wean the reader away from his addiction to reason as were employed by the expressionists.
Reason-dependent characters are shown as fools or deceivers,
operating on a false notion of reality. Readers are forced
to bypass the rational, the orderly and the civilized by
writings which resist being read in a systematic fashion.

Perhaps the most explicit of these contemporary authors
in his championing of the irrational in literature is Julio
Cortázar. Cortázar's fiction is full of characters who,
like the rationalistic fools of Arlt and Discépolo, insist
on submitting all phenomena to logical analysis. The most
famous of these compulsive analyzers is Horacio Oliveira
of *Rayuela* (1963), a character literally unable to refrain
from logical thought. Oliveira's rationalizings bring him
neither satisfaction nor truth, but rather constitute a
pathological addiction. "Me costaba mucho menos pensar que
ser,"[28] he admits. The reader is subjected to long discussions between Oliveira and his similarly-afflicted
friends. These colloquies, *de omnibus rebus et quibusdam
aliis*, confront the reader with all the sins and deficiencies of rational discourse.
     As in expressionist works, one finds an open recognition
of the value of irrational things. The most appealing character in *Rayuela* is a woman who has somehow remained uncon-
taminated by the mania for analysis that characterizes
Oliveira and his friends. Oliveira recognizes the worth of
such a spontaneous approach to life, but reamins stagnated
in his rationalizing and unable to change: "Hay ríos meta-
físicos, ella los nada como esa golondrina está nadando en
el aire...yo describo y defino y deseo esos ríos, ella los
nada. Yo los busco, los encuentro, los miro desde el puente,
ella los nada. Y no lo sabe, igualita a la golondrina...
Ah dejame entrar, dejame ver algún día como ven tus ojos."[29]
The desire to analyze and comprehend appears as an impediment to a satisfactory life.
     Cortázar is also among those writers who purposefully
frustrate the reader intent on approaching literature in
a spirit of logic and order. Much criticism on Cortázar's
work comments on that author's strategies to force readers
to bypass reason as they read the work. One critic, for
instance, says of Cortázar characters: "Si resultan con-
vincentes, aun al lector esteticista, es debido a su fuerza
como signos que intuimos más allá (o mas acá) de nuestra
razón."[30] This critic says of *Rayuela*: "prescindiendo de
la casualidad y de los nexos lógicos, ayuda al lector a
desarrollar otras potencias dormidas en él a causa de la
hipertrofia de la razón."[31] So, like the expressionists
of the *entreguerre*, Cortázar both shows characters abusing
reason and mocks the reader who would read only with his
reason, neglecting to use his intuition and sensibilities.
Cortázar offers frequent homages to the literary innovators
of the period between wars. He acknowledges a major debt
to Roberto Arlt for the intuitive, irrational elements in
his work.[32]
     Numerous other writers of the "boom" years seek to give
a positive value to the irrational, but perhaps none more
strongly than Augusto Roa Bastos (b.1917). Like the expressionists, Roa Bastos shows reason put to perverted uses.
Miguel Vera of *Hijo de hombre* (1960) is a novelistic character whose rational habits of mind have utterly paralyzed
his moral sensibilities. Vera reflects at length on what
he has seen, heard and experienced, yet fails to notice his
own moral inadequacies. The reader, though, finds Vera's
conduct most irresponsible. Vera betrays a heroic character
who seems scarcely to think at all. This suggests the true

hero is one who has not been deformed by the distorting effects of analysis and reflection. Vera, on the other hand, belongs to that class of people of whom a Discépolo character remarks: "La razón no les sirve sino para hacerse irracionales."[33]

Roa Bastos is also representative of those authors who confront the reader with the fatuity of his desire to understand the work rationally. While he is engaged in the reading of *Moriencia* (1969), the reader encounters a severe questioning of that very enterprise: "¿Saben lo que pasa? Se habla demasiado...La palabra es la gran trampa, la palabra vieja, la palabra usada. Es muy cierto eso de que empezamos a morir por la boca como los peces. Yo mismo hablo y hablo. ¿Para qué? Por ahí no se va a ningún lado. Habría que encontrar un nuevo lenguaje, y mejor todavía un lenguaje de silencios en el que nos podamos comunicar por levísimos estremecimientos, como los animales ...por leves alteraciones de esta acumulación de ondas congestionadas que hay en nosotros como un forúnculo a punto de reventar."[34] Deterrents to an overly rational reading abound in Roa Bastos's work: events which cannot be explained in an altogether reasonable and "civilized" manner, startling transitions and the intermingling of "real" events with those which are fantasized or belong to the realm of myth. The reader is not permitted to sort out what is real and what is imagined "Porque hay lo real de lo que no se ve hasta de lo que no existe todavía. Para mí la realidad es lo que queda cuando ha desaparecido toda la realidad, cuando se ha quemado la memoria de costumbre, el bosque que nos impide ver el árbol. Sólo podemos aludirla vagamente, o soñarla, o imaginarla."[35]

Thus, those writers who are the spiritual heirs of expressionism also fulfill Edschmid's injunction to German expressionists: "A house is no longer merely a subject for an artist, consisting of stone, ugly or beautiful; it has to be looked at until its true form has been recognized, until it is liberated from the muffled restraint of a false reality, until everything that is latent within it is expressed."[36] They pry the reader away from his reliance on the things that can most easily be observed, most correctly be measured and most rigorously be analyzed. The reader must be startled, mocked or confounded into abandoning this rationalistic attitude, an attitude inappropriate to the contemplation of "los enigmas centrales del individuo" and "la caótica y oscura condición humana," in Roa Bastos's words.[37]

According to expressionism, the greatest insights come to those characters, narrators and readers who can accept the paradoxical, the ambiguous and the indirect as suitable modes of expression. Those who persist in forcing reality into logical categories merely perpetuate the unworkable notion of a world amenable to rational analysis. The reader of expressionistic literature must learn to see value in discourse which is utterly irrational-sounding, or else he must remain alien to the work and its purposes. For instance, the heroine of *Entre el hierro* displays the greatest acuity when she says "el frío de la comprensión es lo que me sobra" (p. 7) or decries attempts at rational discourse as evasionary tactics. In Arlt's *Los siete locos*, the

Astrologer expounds a thoroughly irrationalistic view of
human existence. Yet he is the character most able to
predict, chart and manipulate the behavior of the others.
Only he and his female companion survive the havoc that
destroys the other characters at the end of *Los lanzallamas,* the sequel to *Los siete locos.* His views are
altogether insightful for the disordered world in which
he operates.

     To be the reader of an expressionistic work, one must
accept the possibility of irrational yet valid insights.
The reader must to some extent bypass rationality and
"civilized" thought in the face of such expressionistic
comments as this one from a Roa Bastos work: "¿Pero qué
es la realidad? Una cebolla. Usted le saca una capa tras
otra, y ¿qué es lo que queda? Nada, pero esa nada es todo,
o por lo menos un tufo picante que nos hace lagrimear los
ojos." [38]

     If the reader refuses to lessen his reliance on logic
and his search for orderly schemata, he may fall victim
to outright mockery on the part of the author. Traps for
too-rational readers are found both in expressionistic
works and in those of the *nueva narrativa.* Some of these
mocking devices appear in the *Historia universal de la
infamia* as discussed above, but many more are found all
through Borges's work of all periods. Carter Wheelock
must preface his monographic study on Borges with a warning
to Borges readers to beware of that author's playful traps
for overly interpretive readers. [39] Similarly, Eduardo
González Lanuza cautions readers of Arlt's Erdosain novels
against attempting too straightforward a reading of those
devious works. Only when the reader has adjusted his
expectations to the expressionistic character of the writings will he be able to read them satisfactorily. [40] A
Cortázar critic suspects that the complicated instructions
for reading *Rayuela* may be "an ironic hoax," since the
novel shows life "without transcendental patterns that
comfort in their all-encompassing mechanisms. The world
of [*Rayuela*] is precisely a world in which this comfort
is lacking, and to adorn its fictional representation with
a spurious pattern is heavy-handed irony against the reader
who follows the directions with passive good faith." [41] If
the work of literature cannot persuade the reader to bypass
the rational and the orderly, it may make sport of his
doggedness. But if the reader will accept the work on its
own expressionistic terms, he may share in its irrational
insights and truths.

     The expressionist subjects his reader to ambiguities,
evasions, confusions, incoherencies and obscure comments
for more than literary reasons. Expressionism seeks to
make the reader aware of those aspects of life to which
reason has blinded him. As Kurt Pinthus put it, expressionism "is all eruption, explosion and intensity--must be,
to break through every hostile crust. Therefore it avoids
naturalistic description of reality...even the war is not
shown with objective realism--it is always shown as a
vision." [42] According to expressionism, the knowledge most
worth having can only be reached by irrational means. One
must persuade the reader to loosen his rationalistic grasp

on reality so that he can perceive not just "descriptions" or "photographs," but "eternal significance," "lived experience" and "visions,"[43] to use Edschmid's words. Expressionism, which "produces its means of expression with mighty, violent energy from the...power of the spirit itself,"[44] confronts man with his own irrational nature and his residence in a world whose truths are not accessible to reason.

ENDNOTES

1. Armando Discépolo, *Entre el hierro*, in his *Obras escogidas*, ed. David Viñas (Buenos Aires: Jorge Alvarez, 1969), I, 25. Further Discépolo page numbers are from this edition.

2. Richard Samuel, and R. Hinton Thomas, *Expressionism in German Life, Literature and the Theatre* (Philadelphia: Albert Saifer, 1971), p. 124.

3. A typical discussion of expressionistic ideas manifested outside the arts is found in Samuel and Thomas, pp. 9-18.

4. Wolfgang Kayser, *Interpretación y análisis de la obra literaria*, 4. ed. rev. (Madrid: Gredos, 1961), p.230.

5. Kayser, p. 193.

6. Walter H. Sokel, *The Writer in Extremis: Expressionism in Twentieth-Century German Literature* (Stanford: Stanford University Press, 1959), p. 66.

7. Sokel, p. 69.

8. Henry Hatfield, *Modern German Literature* (New York: St. Martin's Press, 1967), p. 68.

9. Particularly from Ernesto Sábato's account of these events in his *Hombres y engranajes*, in his *Obras completas* (Buenos Aires: Losada, 1970), II, 141-272.

10. Sábato, preface to his *Obras completas*, II, 12.

11. Sábato, introduction to his *Hombres y engranajes*, in his *Obras completas*, II, 144.

12. Samuel and Thomas, p. 11.

13. Kasimir Edschmid, cited by Samuel and Thomas, p. 11.

14. Julio Cortázar, cited by Evelyn Picon Garfield, *Julio Cortázar* (New York: Ungar, 1975), p. 12.

15. Sábato, *El escritor y sus fantasmas*, in his *Obras completas*, II, 484.

16. Sábato, *El escritor y sus fantasmas*, p. 144.

17. Roberto Arlt, *Los siete locos* (Buenos Aires: Losada, 1968), p. 123.

18. Roberto Arlt, "El desierto entra a la ciudad," in his *Teatro completo*, (Buenos Aires: Schapire, 1969), II, 178. Further Arlt page numbers are from this edition.

19. David Viñas, "Armando Discépolo: grotesco, inmigración y fracaso," introduction to Armando Discépolo, *Obras escogidas,* pp. xxix-xxxi.

20. Viñas, p. xxix.

21. Sokel, p. 66.

22. Hatfield, p. 68.

23. Hannah Arendt, *Eichmann in Jerusalem: a Report on the Banality of Evil* (New York: Viking Press, 1963).

24. Konrad Lorenz, *On Aggression* (New York: Harcourt, Brace and World, 1966).

25. Jorge Luis Borges, *Historia universal de la infamia* (Buenos Aires: Emecé, 1954), p. 17. Further Borges page numbers given in the text are from this edition.

26. Borges, *Ficciones* (Buenos Aires: Emecé, 1956), pp. 33-34.

27. Samuel and Thomas, p. 15.

28. Cortázar, *Rayuela,* 5. ed. (Buenos Aires: Sudamericana, 1967), p. 26.

29. Cortázar, *Rayuela,* p. 116.

30. Lida Aronne Amestoy, *Cortázar: la novela mandala* (Buenos Aires: Fernando García Cambeiro, 1972), p.66.

31. Aronne Amestoy, p. 98.

32. Cortázar, cited by Evelyn Picon Garfield, p. 6.

33. Discépolo, p. 42.

34. ·Augusto Roa Bastos, *Moriencia* (Caracas: Monte Avila, 1969), pp. 63-64.

35. Augusto Roa Bastos, "Imagen y perspectivas de la narrativa latinoamericana actual," in *La novela hispanoamericana,* ed. Juan Loveluck (Santiago de Chile: Editorial Universitaria, 1969), p. 209.

36. Edschmid, cited in Samuel and Thomas, p. 11.

37. Roa Bastos, "Imagen y perspectivas..., p. 209.

38. Roa Bastos, *Moriencia,* pp. 63-64.

39. Carter Wheelock, *The Mythmaker, a Study of·Motif and Symbol in the Short Stories of Jorge Luis Borges* (Austin: University of Texas Press, 1969), p. 12.

40. Eduardo González Lanuza, *Roberto Arlt* (Buenos Aires: Centro Editor, 1971), pp. 88-89.

41. David William Foster, *Currents in the Contemporary Argentine Novel* (Columbia, Missouri: University of Missouri Press, 1975), p. 105.

42. Pinthus, cited by Hatfield, p. 60.

43. Edschmid, cited by Hatfield, p. 59.

44. Pinthus, cited by Hatfield, p. 60.

Chapter 3

Narrative Garble in Expressionism

I

Rejecting the cult of reason, the expressionist posits
the existence of a world not governed by rules and principles that human reason can perceive. With this assumption
about the nature of the world, he must seek a literary
representation adequate to portray and comment upon such
an irrational world. A main tenet of German expressionism
holds that one cannot write about human realities as
though they were logical, but must make his mode of expression suitable to the upheaval in which man lives. For
instance, one section of the famed *Menschheitsdämmerung*
anthology of poets features those whose output is all
"Aufruf und Empörung," and another those who employ the
"Sturz und Schrei."[1] Kurt Pinthus's preface states that
these outcries and ragings are necessary literary devices,
for to "break through every hostile crust" the poet must
use "eruption, explosion, intensity,"[2] To avoid falling
into accustomed, false patterns of perceiving reality, the
movement must "produce its means of expression with mighty,
violent energy."[3] A more orderly presentation risks allowing readers to believe in an orderly, principled cosmos,
exactly the belief which expressionism rejected. Pinthus
describes the expressionists' attempts to find forms of
expression that corresponded to their view of the world:
"Never in world literature did the shriek, the fall, the
longing of an age ring out so loudly, laceratingly, and
startingly...."[4]
The extreme measures that Pinthus championed in his
famous preface came to be the hallmark of German expressionism. Every description of expressionism must empha-
size the fragmented syntax and chaotic structure of the
works produced by that movement. It is easy to characterize expressionistic drama as full of "confused and intense
emotional stammerings,"[5] "distortion of the dramatic
structure,"[6] "plots which are extremely difficult to
follow"[7] and "labyrinths of meditation."[8] Wolfgang Kayser
admits that expressionist drama may initially disconcert
with its "negligencia frente a la unidad de acción y la
ausencia de una estructuración rígida."[9]
However, as Kayser points out, one must recognize these
aberrant features as part of an attempt to convey a certain
view of the universe and its workings. Kayser enjoins the
critic always to view such fragmented works in terms of the
expressionist worldview. The deviant characteristic must
"entenderse mediante una interpretación positiva de la
esencia de cada drama."[10] The expressionists believed that
the truths they needed to express could only be communicated
by a wildly deviant, irrationalistic presentation. Walter
H. Sokel, for instance, justifies some of the more aberrant
elements of expressionism in terms of the expressionists'
belief that "distortion reveals essence."[11] Sokel agrees
that expressionistic works may be puzzling in the extreme,

but points out that Expressionists were not interested in
expressing notions that could be easily assimilated and
understood: "We are here at the crux of the problem of
obscurity in Expressionist and, in general, much of modern
writing. Art is no longer communication."[12] Since the
world did not render up its meaning unambiguously to man's
inquiring mind, it would be false for literature to do so.
Instead, literature ought to confront man with the confusion and ambiguity that was his lot in life.

 Thus, over and over again one finds expressionistic
works that are homologous to the disjointed, enigmatic
universe that they represent. For instance, Georg Kaiser's
1912 drama *Von Morgens bis Mitternachts* may be described
thematically as "satirical allegory: the clerk is an
Everyman lost in a chaotic society which offers only the
choice between the dullest routine and crime."[13] The dramatic representation of this chaotic society is also
chaotic in structure: "The action...moves with frantic
speed.... The bicycle race scene is arch-expressionistic
in its wildly excited crowd and spectacular lighting
effects."[14] Rather than follow its hero's misfortunes
from beginning to end, the play manifests an elliptical
structure characteristic of the so-called "station drama."
It takes this disjointed form because the world it represents is also lacking in unity and logical connections.

 German expressionists had recourse to many devices
meant to make literature incoherent in the same way the
world was incoherent. A very elliptical or fragmentary
presentation, as in *Von Morgens bis Mitternachts,* might
replace linear storytelling. Data necessary to a full
understanding of the plot might be notably missing. For
instance, a critic complains of Victor Sorge's 1910 *Der
Bettler:* "We never learn what specific reason Sorge's
central character had for feeling the need to become a
beggar."[15] Many conflicting notions might be expressed
in the course of a work, none of which would ever emerge
as the "true" one. The spectator or viewer could not
count on a reliable character, a trustworthy narrator or
the events of the plot to confirm or disprove the various
ideas set forth. Of Carl Sternheim's dramas, this comment
is made: "But, as in the case of his expressionist friends,
his total picture of society was confused; his heroes lost
themselves and the audience in labyrinths of meditation,
leaving the audience with no clear idea of what the author
imagined the future to hold for his characters or for
them."[16] Again, if the dramatist holds the world to be an
incoherent, unintelligible place, he may say so by giving
to his works a homologous vagueness and disunity.

 As important as the overall structural dishevelment is
the linguistic deviance typical of expressionistic work.
An historian of the movement summarizes: "The radicals,
however, distorted the language boldly, aiming at a maximum
of dynamism. Accordingly, they expanded the role of the
verb: often verbs are massed together, adjectives or nouns
are transformed to verbs--thus, *monden, nackten*--or adjectives expressing action are coined from verbs: thus 'die
schlafe Erde,' 'den keuchen Tod,...violent words, often
verbal compounds, abound. Traditional punctuation largely

vanishes, although exclamation points are unsurprisingly
rife.... In Stramm, the most extreme of all, grammar
barely survives."[17] Wolfgang Kayser, again, reminds us
that even the most wildly aberrant forms of expression
must be considered as proceeding from the basic tenets of
expressionism: "La lucha contra todas las reglas de
gramatica y contra la tradición terminó, por fin, con el
expresionismo, en una rotura de todos los vínculos lingüísticos y en un balbaceo que ya no era lengua."[18]

The syntactically fragmented poetry described above
finds few equivalents in the works this study discusses.
Although Jorge Luis Borges made an attempt to recreate the
linguistic aberrance and fragmentation of German expressionist poetry in Spanish,[19] most Argentine expressionists
worked in prose fiction and the theater. More germane,
therefore, to this study are the deviant ways in which
characters of expressionist drama expressed themselves,
bypassing rational discourse and straightforward statement.
For instance, a critic states that Franz Wedekind's
"dialogues were couched in an ecstatic language in which
the characters answered one another's unconscious thoughts
rather than their actual words."[20] In *Frühlings Erwachsen*,
first produced in 1906, a Wedekind character speaks entirely
in riddles. A commentator characterizes the worst of
expressionist drama: "the characters could...stand forth
and overwhelm the fascinated onlookers by their screams of
anguish and revolt."[21] All these deviant features point to
a desire to avoid reasoned conversation, excessively neat
explanations and a reassuring predominance of "civilized"
discourse. The spectator must grasp the meaning of the
play, and indeed the meaning of life, by intuitive, irrational, even "primitive" faculties latent in man.

Argentine expressionism, like the European *fontis ab
qua* it flows, seeks to create a work of literature homologous in form to the universe it represents. As in the
case of the German expressionists, the Latin American
writers posited the existence of an incoherent universe,
whose workings were not to be understood by rational inquiry and whose truths were not to be transmitted by
rational discourse. Literature must dissuade the reader
from his reliance on ratiocination and his insistence on
being fully informed. It must persuade him to accept the
irrational, the unexplained and the anomalous as predom-
inant features of human existence, not to be explained away
by a vigorous application of reason. Therefore, literature must refrain from presenting the reader with a fictional world more well-ordered than the world that we
inhabit.

So we find Argentine expressionists resorting to many
of the same disordering literary devices used by German
expressionists. Data seemingly important to the understanding of the plot is omitted. Contradictory notions
appear without any indication of which is more valuable
or more correct. Characters and narrators forego a
straightforward presentation of their statements, resorting
to riddles, ambiguities, evasions, poetic effusions and
unintelligible remarks. One character, Arlt's Astrologer,

communicates partly by means of charades and news reports that have been fabricated for some rhetorical end. The overall structure of the work lacks unity and coherence. Frequently the time sequence is unclear, and it may be unclear whether some events take place at all, are imagined, fabricated or hallucinated. These formal devices reinforce the thematic assertions of expressionism concerning the nature of man's universe.

II

Roberto Arlt's deviant expression, long ascribed to his lack of education, leisure or personal stability, is now becoming recognized as a manifestation of Latin American expressionism.[22] For instance, it is by now a commonplace that Arlt's Erdosain novels, *Los siete locos* (1929) and *Los lanzallamas* (1931) are only superficially crime novels and fail to satisfy the exigencies of that genre. Commentaries on Arlt's work may list a number of "loose ends" in the plot, occurrences that are never fully explained or that appear inverisimilar in terms of other events in the story. The reader is thus alerted that he must read these apparent thrillers in quite a different spirit from that of the "armchair detective" or skilled reader of detective stories.[23]

Going beyond this rather obvious lack of complete explanations for all occurrences, we find Arlt using a number of devices to undermine the reader's confidence in what the narrator has to tell him. Especially disconcerting is the use of footnotes that contradict the statements to which they refer. Such a footnote is appended to an episode occurring in a meeting of revolutionaries. The Astrologer, as leader of the cabal, introduces a new member as the Major, explaining that the man holds that rank in the Argentine military. Shortly thereafter, he announces that the Major is a mere civilian, introduced as a major in order to demonstrate the superiority of appearance over reality. The Astrologer's revelation is glossed, though, with the statement that the Astrologer first gave the man's true identity and then lied when he claimed to have lied about it.[24] The footnotes and the text itself are both the words of the same narrator, a man who has taken it upon himself to reconstruct and chronicle the events of Erdosain's last days. Thus this self-appointed historian is telling the reader not to believe a statement that he himself has included in the text proper. The question of the Major's identity does not come up again in the novels. Such unresolved confusion frustrates any reader who attempts to read the novels as one would a novel of crime and detection. The matter of the Major's identity is a puzzle that simply has no solution.

"El traje del fantasma," a 1933 short story, again uses the footnote apparently to clarify a point, but really in order to create confusion. The text is an accused murderer's own account of the fantastic circumstances that will explain his connection with the corpse found in his room. His stated intention is to convince the reader that he did not kill the man and was not, as the popular press would have it, the dead man's lover. He asserts that a

rapid succession of fantastic events befell him, including
a sojourn in a land of skeletons. At the end of the accused man's deposition, a footnote appears. It warns the
reader that the man's account is nothing more than an
attempt to appear mad and thus escape responsibility for
the murder.[25] The reader has no indication whose work the
footnote is. Thus he can equally well believe the footnote's statement that the prisoner was feigning madness or
the prisoner, who says he does not want to be thought mad.
If the footnote is wrong and the prisoner's deposition is
a sincere effort, the events of the narrative may still be
seen in more than one way. They may be not deliberately
fabricated untruths, but rather the recollection of a series
of hallucinations. If the story is a genuinely fantastic
one, the prisoner's amazing story may have happened much
as he tells it. Not only is the reader left unsure whether
he has been reading clever lies, remembered hallucinations
or fantastic adventures, but he is also unsure whether the
story is principally naturalistic--the sordid tryst and
subsequent murder, the workings of the criminal mind--or
whether fantastic elements predominate, like the suspension
of normal time and space, the voyage to a land populated
by skeletons and the magic forces that determine the course
of events. Through the highly ambiguous relationship
between footnote and text, the entire tale becomes the
indecipherable expression of a disordered universe, the
world-as-madhouse of expressionism.

The footnote is also a device serving to decrease the
reader's awareness of the fictional status of the work. At
one point, ten days in Erdosain's life are left unaccounted
for in the narrative. A footnote tells us that the narrator acknowledges this gap in his chronicle. He claims,
however, to have heard Erdosain's account of those missing
days, an account that would fill another book. Although
considerations of space preclude immediate disclosure of
that material, the narrator holds out to the reader the
possibility of a disclosure "posiblemente algún día."[26]
Another footnote again suggests the existence of a body of
material that has been withheld from the reader. One character has on his person a book of personal musings which
may shed light on the part he plays in the events of the
plot. As the text makes it clear how revealing the contents
of that notebook may prove to be, a footnote is appended.
The footnote says "En la segunda parte de este libro daremos
un extracto de la libreta de Barsut."[27] These two footnotes
do not contradict what has been said in the text itself.
Rather they violate one's common-sense notion that characters in a work of fiction cannot have any existence outside that work. One can be certain of that idea and yet
be tricked into believing that Erdosain has had ten days
of activity that would fill an entire volume, or that
Barsut's notebook was known to the narrator, but that this
information is inaccessible to the reader. The narrator
is himself a fiction, but he pretends to have more reality
than his tale and to be able to withhold parts of his story
when he feels so inclined. The reader can be convinced
momentarily that this fictional being knows more about the
characters in the novel than any mere reader can know.

In addition, footnotes that really do serve to clarify appear in the same text with the spurious ones. For instance, the publisher leaves a note to explain an obscure period reference[28] and the author notes that he elaborated his plot before the occurrences of the sixth of September 1930, rather than fictionalizing history.[29] The existence of such straightforward notes alongside those meant to generate confusion makes the reader even more suspicious, to use Nathalie Sarraute's word.[30]

Arlt's novels violate our notion that a story should be told in an elegant, accessible manner and should present narrative data at a moment when it will illuminate the emerging plot and its overall significance. The Arltian novel may either move too swiftly to facilitate comprehension or proceed so slowly as to cast doubt on the competence of the narrator. The Erdosain novels open and close with dispatch, but at various moments the story becomes becalmed amid a great deal of data that bear no obvious relation to the story proper.

For instance, Haffner's death agony occupies an entire chapter in *Los lanzallamas*. At this juncture in the plot, the reader is most eager to know why the conspirators have decided to eliminate Haffner. Indeed, Erdosain's motivation for deciding others shall die is a highly ambiguous point throughout the two novels and one that has attracted considerable critical attention. The reader would reasonably look to the description of Haffner's last moments for some clarification of this matter. After all, it is conventional in crime novels for betrayed gang members to name their murderers before dying. But in Arlt the reader is subjected instead to a rambling account of Haffner's life as a procurer. The account runs to great detail, such as how Haffner locked one prostitute out on a balcony all one winter night and failed to kill her in this fashion. This welter of trivia makes more evident the absence of any information relevant to the decision to murder Haffner. The insigificant is continually substituted for what is central and significant.

In the narration of Erdosain's death we find another such substitution. The plot is interrupted by a passage explaining how that character's unhappy childhood left him forever alienated. Not only has the reader had ample evidence of Erdosain's unhappiness and alienation, but he has already been told the story of Erdosain's childhood. One may well wonder why such a redundant passage should occur at the last moment before Erdosain's death. At the same time, information the reader wants is being withheld: why Erdosain acquired a stupid, cross-eye mistress by degrading means, maintained her despite the revulsion she inspired in him and suddenly murdered her. The only purpose of this tardy retelling of Erdosain's early life is to be as painfully pointless as Erdosain's life was.

A third instance of irrelevant information encumbering the narrative occurs when Erdosain's wife, Elsa, leaves him. Taking refuge in a convent, she tells the story of her unhappy marriage to the nuns, for catharsis and to justify leaving the marriage. Elsa's account forms a chapter in *Los lanzallamas*. The chapter offers a fresh point of view

on Erdosain's difficulties. However, Elsa proves to be
another wildly erratic narrator. Like the unreliable
central narrator of the novels, she congests her story with
unimportant details and omits significant connections between events. She shares the central chronicler's disin-
clination to distinguish between what matters and what is
peripheral. She violates our notion that there is a hier-
archy of importance in which some things must be said and
recognized, while others are less essential.

For instance, Elsa describes the stay of a young
prostitute, Erdosain's guest, in their household. Of this
stressful period, Elsa chooses to remember the difficulties
she experienced trying to provide the girl with footwear
and apparel. Elsa also mentions that one morning the girl
began rooting aimlessly about in a little strip of soil
near the house. This story, surely a peripheral anecdote,
is related in detail. One learns how the girl acquired a
digging tool and how Elsa tried to impose cosmos on chaos
by suggesting the girl turn her rooting behavior into the
cultivation of lettuce and tomatoes. Elsa mentions only
briefly her conviction that the girl was eager to murder
her reluctant benefactress, although most readers would
consider murderous intention more important than vegetable
gardening.

Elsa's too-detailed treatment of this episode bears
witness to the severity of the girl's derangement. The
world must be, indeed, a disordered place to produce such
irrational behavior in young people. Yet the world's
disorder manifests itself in a more alarming fashion in
Elsa's mode of storytelling. Elsa is, after all, one of
the more conventionally sane characters in the novels;
one critic has called her "la típica burguesita" for her
adherence to existing norms.[31] Thus if shoes, stockings,
lettuce and tomatoes merit more attention in her story
than does intent to commit murder, something very basic
has gone awry. The general breakdown of values and beliefs
that the novel depicts has swept away the devices by which
human beings make sense of the world.

III

Paradoxically, some of the most disorienting passages
in Arlt's fiction adhere superficially to generally-
accepted norms for storytelling. In the context of a
literary work that is often narrated in a wildly aberrant
fashion, such conventionally related passages provoke yet
further suspicion. The reader is given no indication in
what spirit to read these apparently straightforward sec-
tions. One of Arlt's fictional conspirators describes
this perplexing strategy in terms of chess. The character
describes a chessmaster's genius as "elasticidad del
juego." By this he means that the player "no debe tomar
un solo final del juego, sino muchos...porque así descon-
cierta de cien maneras al adversario."[32] Indeed, the reader
of Arlt finds himself the adversary of a narrator who will
allow his purposes and goals to be grasped.

An example of such elasticity is the ending of Los
lanzallamas. At first, the novel seems to draw to a close
in a slow and eccentric manner. Erdosain's death is twice

related, once as perceived by the sensational press and then in a more leisurely and accurate version reconstructed by the chronicler. The second telling includes elements that contradict the popular notion of how a wanted criminal must die. In the chronicler's version, Erdosain's mild appearance disturbs onlookers, for it disrupts their way of thinking about crime: "La sorpresa de la policía al constatar que aquel joven pálido y delicado era el feroz asesino Erdosain no es para ser descripta."[33] Erdosain seems to have died absorbed by the effort to remain decorously upright, rather than by reflections on the events that led to his death. Further incongruity comes with the appearance of an old man who spits on the dead Erdosain, pronouncing this curse and elegy: "Hijo de puta. Tanto coraje mal empleado."[34]

While the narrator has up to this point been emphasizing the outlandish or disturbing aspects of Erdosain's death, he suddenly begins to tell his story in an especially conventional manner. He reveals briefly what happened to each of the other conspirators after Erdosain's death. Certainly it is a well-established novelistic convention to make known the fates of the various characters before closing. However, in a novel that withholds so much key information about its characters, such an abundance of specific information is puzzling.

However, the manner in which the story ends still precludes the reader's answering important questions: did the members of the cabal truly intend to put their revolutionary schemes into practice, and were they competent to do so? The newest recruits, who share the reader's curiosity, question senior members on these points. The answers they receive are enigmatic and evasive, not informative. One member admits the revolutionary plans may be ill-founded, but "Ya que la vida no tiene sentido, es igual seguir cualquier corriente."[35] The Astrologer answers Barsut's persistent questioning thus: "Yo sé que no puede ser, pero hay que proceder como si fuera factible."[36] On another occasion he responds to a question about the possible failure of his plan with the words "los que pagarán serán ustedes, no yo."[37]

Nor will the reader find a more definitive answer in the unfolding events of the plot. A swift succession of reverses results in the death, capture or disappearance of the cell members. Their grandiosely-elaborated schemes to foment insurgency are never put to the test. Thus it remains unclear whether these plans were intended to be carried out and whether the cell members could have been successful active revolutionaries.

Another question that has no one definitive answer is that of the precise nature of the characters' difficulties. Again, the characters themselves pose the problem to one another, formulating only cryptic answers in reply. Asked to provide an explanation for his erratic behavior, Erdosain says: "Uno roba, hace macanas porque está angustiado."[38] He tells a questioner that the source of his unwise behavior is precisely "lo que yo no sé."[39]

Critics, less willing than Erdosain to abandon the search for ultimate causes, have argued that the Arltian character suffers from the breakdown of the lower middle class, the loss of faith in God, existential terror, immigrant malaise, unresolved Oedipal complexes and simple poverty. Indeed, evidence can be found throughout Arlt's works to substantiate all of these diagnoses.

To examine this highly complex and ambiguous issue, let us reduce it to two simpler problems involved in specifying the nature of this Arltian uneasiness. To what extent does economic deprivation underlie the characters' unhappiness and to what extent is the urban environment at fault?

Economic wellbeing appears as both the *sine qua non* of happiness and a factor insufficient to bring satisfaction. A wealthy benefactor is the agent of fulfillment in Erdosain's recurring fantasies. In one version, a millionairess resolves his marital distress by pensioning off Erdosain's wife and taking the weary husband on a cruise to tropical lands. In another an eccentric millionaire ends Erdosain's career frustrations by agreeing to underwrite all his inventions. Elsa equates economic security with not only contentment, but with personal adequacy: "Remo es suficiente hombre para ganar para nosotros dos," she rebukes a would-be benefactor.[40] To justify abandoning Erdosain at a stressful moment in his life, she shows him her hands, witness to life without servants.

However, money brings Erdosain less fulfillment in reality than in his imaginings. He spends an embezzled sum "de una manera absurda,"[41] contracting prostitutes of whom he requires nothing, purchasing luxuries he does not enjoy and yet not replacing his worn-out apparel. In an excess of despair, he treads a sum of money underfoot, finding no solace in what he once desired. Erdosain's musings on his unsatisfied needs for divine and for human communication cause many critics to consider him an existential hero. Mirta Arlt, for instance, places Erdosain within "las coordenadas del hombre existencial de nuestro tiempo,"[42] in the line of Sartre's Saint Genet.

Similarly, the urban environment appears as both a genuine hell and as a convenient target for the characters' complaints. The best argument for the former point of view is made by Stasys Gostautas in his "La evasión de la ciudad en las novelas de Roberto Arlt." Gostautas finds in Arlt's work the most trenchant statement of *menosprecio de corte y alabanza de aldea* since the writings of Fray Luis de León.[43] He cites numerous instances of characters ascribing their problems to the unnatural rigors of city life.

However, one may also find examples of country life failing to satisfy. Hipólita, for instance, is a character who has carried out the fantasy of living in the provinces. She was horrified by what she witnessed there: "Era una vida bestial la de esta gente." Hipólita found that provincials "juzgaban los casamientos y los noviazgos por el número de hectáreas que sumaban...entre ellos, sentí que mi vida agonizaba precozmente, peor que cuando vivía en el más incierto de los presentes de la ciudad." The Astrologer agrees with these opinions: "El dinero y la política es la única verdad para la gente de nuestro campo."[44] The cell's revolutionary plans depend on the greed, gullibility, boredom and other negative features of the rural population. None of the conspirators objects to such an unflattering

characterization of rural life, although it is hardly con-
sonant with the notion that country living fosters spiritual purity.

In short, ambiguity is inherent in the characters'
misery. At moments they believe that pastoral settings
will revive their flagging spiritual energies. At other
times, they accept a highly negative portrayal of country
living. The events of the plot offer no indication as to
which view is truer. Gostautas cites characters who believe
the country could heal them. However, these characters are
Arltian characters, masters of self-deception, self-contra-
diction and obfuscation. They do not realize their longings
to live in a rural setting, so we cannot know whether a
pastoral environment would have eased their anxieties.
Again, the reader is left with too little definite information to decide how matters really stand in the plot.

IV

Arlt's fiction also disconcerts the reader by appearing, at various moments, to belong to various varieties of
prose fiction. The reader may make a classification that
shortly turns out to be more illusory than real. In some
cases the resemblance is altogether deceptive, for the Arlt
work is radically unlike the form it superficially follows.
In other cases, what is surprising is the multiple classifications to which one Arltian work lends itself, all
categorizations having a certain validity, but none the
definitive characterization. The reader is put off his
guard by his inability to presuppose what the fiction will
"really" be about, what rules it will follow and in what
spirit he ought to approach it.

For instance, *Los siete locos* and *Los lanzallamas*
exhibit certain features of the naturalistic or documentary-
realistic novel. They do provide, to a certain extent,
information about a certain social milieu at a certain
moment. One critic finds in these novels a depiction of
the stress experienced by those who found it difficult to
remain in the middle class. In his analysis, the characters are torn between their need to present themselves
as solidly middle class and the economic impossibility of
doing so. He cites instances of sudden downward mobility,
with its disorienting effect on the characters.[45]

However, the novels break with the conventions of
realism early on. As *Los siete locos* opens, Erdosain has
embezzled a sum of money from his firm, which now knows of
the crime. Called to account for his misdeed, Erdosain
must surely, if he is a realistic character, plead dire
necessity. Indeed, his clothes are ragged, his wife complains of his improvidence and he has no furniture in his
house. Yet the embezzled funds went not to satisfy material
needs, but rather to fulfill some obscure spiritual exigency.
"Nunca se me ocurrió comprarme botines con este dinero,"
he says, to which the narrator adds: "Y era cierto. El
placer que experimentó en un principio de disponer impune-
mente de lo que no le pertenecía se evaporó pronto."[46]
Certainly no realistically-portrayed character would act
according to the demands of some undefined inner prompting,
spending the stolen money capriciously. Thus Erdosain

demonstrates to the reader that he is no ordinary realistic hero and that his difficulties are not altogether societal in origin.

After this initial display of deviance, Erdosain shows himself to have many problems suitable to the hero of a realistic work: his wife abandons him, apparently for a wealthier man, his job as a clerk is trivial and alienating, he cannot afford to develop working models of his inventions and he has poverty-induced tuberculosis. Yet his responses to these problems are atypical and disconcerting. When he finds his wife preparing to abandon him, just as he has been found out as an embezzler, he displays little outward despair or anger. Instead, he engages his wife's new protector, an army officer, in a discussion of his various inventions and proposed reforms. As Erdosain digresses onto such topics as his unhappy childhood and his scheme to market many-colored dogs, the officer gives every sign of being bored and unreceptive. Yet Erdosain continues to confess his innermost thoughts and most shameful experiences to this uncaring military man. The scene ends with Erdosain and his wife elaborating a fantasy of reunion, seemingly oblivious to the officer's presence. Any initial resemblance to realistic fiction is undermined and destroyed by this barrage of irrational behavior.

Arlt's prefatory remarks may create false expectations in the reader. For instance, the often-cited introduction to *Los lanzallamas* seems to be the apologia for an unflinching attempt to document certain unpleasant societal realities at the expense of esthetic considerations. Arlt satirizes an imagined reviewer's reaction: "El señor Arlt sigue aferrado a su realismo de pésimo gusto."[47] The concern of the responsible author, according to this introduction, must be "los ruidos de un edificio social que se desmorona," not "bordados."[48] Arlt includes himself among those who create "nuestra literatura, no conversando continuamente de literatura, sino escribiendo en orgullosa soledad libros que encierran la violencia de un 'cross' a la mandíbula."[49] Similarly, Arlt dedicates *El jorobadito* to his wife with another apology for his esthetic sins, citing again the exigencies of honesty. While he would have liked to write a literarily satisfying work, he says, he could not in good conscience falsify human realities with "doradas palabras mentirosas," but rather must remain "en contacto con gente terrestre, triste y somnolienta."[50] Arlt seems to proclaim his adherence to the established tenets of social realism by his words of introduction. The aberrance of the works that follow thus become all the more startling as they violate these very tenets.

The beginnings of stories or of episodes in novels may also make one expect a particular kind of relation to follow, only to turn into something very different indeed. For instance, the title story in *El jorobadito* appears at first to be the anguished outpourings of an accused murderer who remains convinced that he has rid the world of an evil being. The narrator then proves most inept at substantiating his own thesis. While he gives many serious instances of his own cruelty to the murdered hunchback, his only example of the victim's alleged evil is the man's alleged beating of a sow. This eccentric, almost frivolous charge, never elaborated upon, suggests the narrator is an erratic, unreliable individual. One wonders how seriously to take his anguish or his claim to have vanquished an evil by killing his deformed friend.

The narrator further destroys the reader's confidence by departing entirely from his argument that his crime was justifiable. He relates instead the horrors of a middle-class engagement to a proper, chaperoned girl. Now his denunciation seems to shift from the evil in the world, represented by the hunchback, to the hypocrisy of a certain social milieu, exemplified by his fiancee and her vigilant mother. Only at the story's end do the two threads converge. Against the protests of the hunchback, the narrator insists his fiancee's first kiss be not for him but for the deformed man, as proof her love is stronger than revulsion and propriety. While the divergent elements of the plot meet, literally, the main rhetorical thrust of the story is still unclear. Does he care more to tell us about his justifiable crime or to show us the grotesque conventions of courtship and marriage? The reader is as bewildered as the audience of a German expressionist work in which numerous themes appear, develop in an erratic manner and come to no clear resolution. The world's disorder is not set to rights as part of the creation of a fictional universe. In fact, the unwieldiness of the literary work exceeds that of the real world in order to more firmly impress upon the reader the existence of unresolvable confusions.

The narrator of the stories in *El criador de gorilas* also raises expectations about his story that he does not fulfill. Though the stories at first resemble adventure stories in exotic settings, expressionistic confusions soon intrude. The narrator of the title story ostensibly sets out to give an eyewitness account of mutiny against the gorilla raiser. To this end he documents atrocities supposedly perpetrated by the gorilla breeder against his employees. Soon incongruous and whimsical elements make one doubt the reliability of the witness. The narrator, applying for work at the breeder's, is given a bottle of liquor and instructions to become drunk. The breeder finds his new employee three days later and, apparently satisfied with his drunkenness, gives him further orders. The horrendous or scabrous particulars of life on the gorilla farm occupy a prominent place in the relation, as does the narrator's insistence on his own unregenerate character. The chronology of the story is awry; the hiring anecdote follows several occurrences that the narrator could only have witnessed after gaining access to the farm.

One further doubts the value of the documentation of atrocities when the narrator commits a startling redundancy. After he has described in lurid detail the gorilla breeder's death, he informs the reader that "se lo comían vivo las hormigas."[51] This event can hardly have escaped one's attention, and its reiteration seems to confirm the unbalanced nature of the narrator and the ramshackle construction of the world he inhabits.

Not only do Arlt's works confound one by conforming to and then violating the conventions of some familiar

form, but they resist classification by conventional genres.
It is frequently observed that *El juguete rabioso*, Arlt's
1926 novel, has more the features of a collection of short
stories.[52] Conversely, while *El jorobadito* is in format a
book of short stories, Arlt himself refers to it as one of
his novels.[53] Indeed, the stories comprising it are closely
linked by their urban settings, violent action and by the
absence of a dependable narrative voice. The stories are
all related in an exceedingly fragmented, cryptic and often
chaotic fashion. Deformity, whether physical, spiritual
or moral, is a constant theme in the stories; thus the
title invites the reader to see them as all part of one
fragmented portrait of societal and personality disintegration.

Moreover, it is difficult to say whether the 1929 *Los
siete locos* and the 1931 *Los lanzallamas* constitute one
novel or two. The two texts deal with the same characters
and revolutionary conspiracy. Yet they have separate
titles, and are not designated as parts one and two. *Los
siete locos* presents difficulties to the reader by presenting the characters and plot situation in a sketchy,
piecemeal and ambiguous manner. In *Los lanzallamas*, the
plot is already set forth. Other, less esthetically in-
triguing difficulties greet the reader. Most notable of
these is the exceedingly tortured syntax of certain passages.
The latter novel also stuns one by including long political
harangues by the Astrologer and Erdosain's plans and schemata for a poison gas factory, documents unlikely to have
meaning for readers.

That the novels both are two halves of one work and
two separate entities is the basis of an Arltian caprice.
The Astrologer is left, at the end of *Los siete locos*, sitting speechless over a comparison between him and Lenin.
Los lanzallamas whimsically opens with the Astrologer's
reaction, which he has finally managed to verbalize: "Sí,
pero Lenín sabía adónde iba."[54] Through this ploy, which
strikes some readers as too frivolous,[55] Arlt emphasizes
the ambiguous status of the two texts: one more feature
of his fiction which can never be fully grasped or defined.

All of these devices serve to prevent the reader from
feeling he can determine what exactly he is reading and
how he is to read it. The reader does not know many things
he would like to know about the erratically unfolding plot.
Nor does he know why he is given other bits of information
that strike him as trivial or peripheral. He does not know
to what extent he can believe the chronicler of the conspiracy in the Erdosain novels, nor who this chronicler
is. Narrators in other Arlt works also exhibit erratic
behavior that casts doubt on the veracity of their statements. Among the devices that indicate this irresponsi-
bility are the use of footnotes that contradict the text
or seem to violate the autonomy of the work, conventionally
related passages juxtaposed with those of a wildly disordered nature, the creation of false expectations in the
reader and puzzling redundancies. In short, the form of
the work of literature becomes as haphazard and baffling
as the form of the world it represents: the expressionistic world-as-madhouse.

V

Although Arlt is often a difficult writer, particularly in the tortuous syntax and lengthy digressions of *Los lanzallamas,* his work is accessible in other ways. While the main focus of the Erdosain novels may shift with disconcerting swiftness, one can still see that they are "about" alienation, marginality, anomie, spiritual rootlessness and other spiritual, societal and psychological woes. It is also clear that a conspiracy forms about a charismatic leader who gives each member a feeling of purpose and wholeness that he cannot find outside the group. A recognizable plot exists: Erdosain becomes involved ever more deeply with the cabal; other members are incorporated, allowing the reader some insight into the dynamics of the secret society; finally, the plotters are disbanded by violent death and police pursuit. Though not allowed to grasp fully the workings of the Arltian fictional world, one does gain some understanding of its main preoccupations.

Much more disorienting is a body of literary work that lacks such comforts as plot, characters and themes in the usual sense. These reassuringly familiar elements have been eliminated from the work of Macedonio Fernández. The works of this innovator are still being discovered and published as a result of his belated, post-boom recognition.

This production is difficult to classify for, as Adolfo de Obieta says, "Toda la obra de M.F. pudo llamarse Miscelánea, modesta palabra preciosamente connatural al cosmos. Misceláneas mayores, menores, ínfimas...."[56] Nonetheless one work, *Museo de la novela de la Eterna* (1967), stands out for its relative unity. It is a work that stands in some enigmatic relationship to the novel and comments upon that genre. Noé Jitrik, considering the ambiguous status of this curious text, states that it is "en gran medida el objeto en el que la 'Estética de la novela' se hace al mismo tiempo forma de una novela."[57] However, Jitrik chooses not to analyze the work as one would a novel, even though it might be "metodológicamente correcto" to do so. Instead he examines it as something approaching a manifesto about the making of a new novel "porque lo que en definitiva Macedonio afirma es una cierta escritura, lingüísticamente considerada, más que una 'novela' realmente posible."[58] That Jitrik considers studying the text as a novel, though, is witness to the double nature of *Museo de la novela de la Eterna.* It is a work that challenges and disturbs one's received notion of what literary genre is and how a work's genre is determined.

Museo de la novela de la Eterna is the most unified of the author's works. The other writings are not only difficult to classify but also exceedingly fragmented. The 1928 *No toda es vigilia la de los ojos abiertos* was characterized by its author as a collection of philosophical writings. However, commentators have found it more difficult to categorize than that, for its treatment of philosophical ideas is far from philosophy by any orthodox sense. Jitrik speaks of "el general impulso a la filosofía de que Macedonio había dado ya herméticas pruebas en su *No toda es vigilia la de los ojos abiertos*."[59] Though Macedonio's incursions into philosophy are unorthodox, Jitrik does not consider them to be ironic, but earnest: "Macedonio Fernández, cuya obra es un acto de fe en la inteligencia," he writes.[60] Other critics find the treatment of ideas in the writings highly ironic and devoid of faith. Jean Franco, for instance, speaks of Macedonio's "playing games with serious ideas"[61] while Germán L. García characterizes the author as a writer who conceived of himself as a philosopher.[62] The way in which Macedonio addresses himself to philosophical problems is so unlike what one considers serious philosophy that it is easy to conclude he has abandoned all intellectual rigor or is being completely ironic. Again, the very nature of the work is ambiguous and therefore disconcerting. While in *Museo de la novela de la Eterna* one may be reading either fiction or erratically presented literary theory. *No toda es vigilia la de los ojos abiertos* may be an earnest attempt to approach the universe through intelligence or a mocking imitation of that very attempt.

Other parts of Macedonio's literary work will never appear in print because they are designed to bypass the written word entirely. We know of them only through descriptions provided by the author or by friends to whom he elaborated his projects for unwritten novels. One such novel, conceptualized but never realized, would have used Macedonio's friends as characters, thus eliminating the need for verbally-created characters. The fictional setting would not be created with words, either; rather Buenos Aires would be cast in this role. While such conceptual works have no material existence, they are in a sense part of Macedonio's total literary achievement. Like his written works, they challenge one's notions of what a literary work ought to offer its readers.

In short, Macedonio's literary production puzzles and shocks by its accurate identification of the features we most expect to find in a literary work and corresponding refusal to supply those elements. The criticism on these anomalous works points to various norms that are deliberately disregarded. As Jitrik says, "en todas partes, Macedonio viola alguna norma."[63] Macedonio draws attention to this aspect of his achievement in the title and main conceit of his 1929 *Papeles de recienvenido*. In these short whimsical essays, the narrative voice is that of a "recienvenido al mundo literatio"[64] who looks at all literary matters, as well as other things, with fresh eyes. Lacking the normal presuppositions about what literary efforts ought to be like, the newcomer comes into conflict with those who have mastered these assumptions. For instance, he finds it unreasonable of the magazine *Martín Fierro* to insist on "sólo artículos cercados o sea contenidos por un cerco y que tuvieran la solución cerca, y, además, que ocuparan un solo lugar."[65] Simple editorial requirements elicit startling responses from the newcomer. He fails to observe the convention by which authors ignore certain aspects of their relationship with the reader. Thus, when asked for a brief note, the newcomer thinks of a compromise solution: "Todo lo que puedo es empezarlos

cortos. En este esfuerzo he logrado hacer de mis primeros
cuatro renglones una reconocida notoriedad de brevedad.
Está debidamente codificada entre todos los lectores del
mundo la regla de ausentarse después de la cuarta línea;
a esta altura cuando yo leo, suspendo; cuando escribo,
sigo, pero justificadamente, pues la brevedad ya la he
satisfecho al principio."[66] Such statements at first sound
merely capricious in their violation of logic, good sense
and convention. Yet, it is not much more absurd for a
writer to assume that all readers will read only four lines
of his work than for him to assume that all readers will
read all of his words with care, finding meaning in all of
them.

Not only here but throughout his writings Macedonio
suggests that writing and reading may be much more arbitrary, disordered and unsystematic activities than we would
like to imagine. In his Museo de la novela de la Eterna,
he celebrates those readers who, bored by an interminable
series of prologues, forewarnings and introductions, have
been skipping parts of the text: "Al lector salteado me
acojo."[67] Indeed, he accuses word-for-word readers of
lack of imagination and excessive faith in the well-ordered
and tidy. He scolds: "¿No te infunde pavura y entristece
tu orientación en el arte que practicas de ensartar un día
tras otro llanamente de tu sólida cotidianidad que te hace
cenar plácido cada noche pensando en el almuerzo del día
siguiente...."[68] Clearly, those who have recourse to art
ought to be more aware of the paradoxical, the irrational
and the eccentric as essential parts of living. One ought
to read elipticallly, to practice "el entreleer,"[69] because,
paradoxically, "los personajes y los sucesos sólo insinu-
ados, hábilmente truncos, son los que más quedan en la
memoria."[70]

The notion that an arbitrary reading, supplemented by
the reader's imagination, is the best one has been carried
over into Macedonian criticism. Germán García, in his
1975 study Macedonio Fernández: la escritura en objeto,
refuses to specify where his quotations may be found in the
various writings of the author under discussion. To follow
this normal pattern of documentation would, he feels, en-
courage readers already inclined to pursue a linear, orderly,
principled reading of the works. Admitting that the refusal
to document the source of quotes is a curious critical innovation, the critic justifies himself in terms of a hoped-
for effect on the reader. "El truco consiste," he asserts,
"en proponer al lector que lea todos los textos en cualquier
orden y de cualquier manera."[71]

The narrator of Museo de la novela de la Eterna, the
literary newcomer and other Macedonian narrators have recourse to a variety of ploys to push the reader toward a
more eccentric, disordered reading. It is frequently
assumed that the reader will side with the newcomer and
oppose the editorial boards with which the eccentric essayist has difficulties. The narrator pleads his case to the
reader: "Por diminuto que sea un trabajo debe empezar.
Pero los Directores no lo entienden así; no pueden ver que
un artículo empiece. Es un alarmismo tal que sólo se
tranquilizan de que no será largo si uno les promete no
comenzarlo."[72] The reader can be counted on to see the jus-

tice of the narrator's side of the argument, because the narrator and readers have not been deformed by the peculiar conventions of "normal" literature. "Me parece que yo hago como todos,"[73] the newcomer says as self-justification.

The narrator of *Museo de la novela de la Eterna* also presupposes a readership as original and untrammeled by convention as himself. He optimistically asserts that no reader of his can be so stodgy as to attempt a linear reading: "Confío en que no tendré lector seguido. Sería el que puede causar mi fracaso...."[74] Suspecting, nonetheless, the existence of such convention-bound readers, the narrator attempts to win them over to the esthetic virtues of randomness and disorder. Those who have already adopted a haphazard style of reading are assured that they have chosen well: "no quise corregirte porque al contrario eres el lector sabio, pues que practicas el entreleer que es lo que más fuerte impresión labra."[75] He expresses his solidarity with those who bypass the conventional notions of reading: "El lector salteado es el más expuesto conmigo a leer seguido," he says,[76] since reading and writing will achieve a perfect fit with one another. It is to these random readers that the novel is dedicated.[77]

Opposed to the eccentric esthetics of the reader and narrator are the forces of literary convention, which appear from time to time to demand that the narrator curb his innovations. These forces are seen as humorless, authoritarian and disagreeable: "La comunicación de los directores no dice si avisarán cuando estén de mejor humor; no usan posdatas que alegren. Si insisto me van a prosperar hacia la calle."[78] Their demands for rigor and order result in the trivialization of literary life. For instance, the newcomer tries to upgrade the publication to which he contributes: "En los días en que toda la literatura es 'Señor, habiéndose derretido la ley de alquileres, prefiera usted, desde hoy, en esta su casa por esa mi casa, pagarme 80 pesos más, etc.', me dirigí a 'Martín Fierro' pidiéndole me aumentaran espacio para los escritos."[79] Those who control literary life, however, are bound by such constraints as considerations of space, financing and what has always been done. They give the newcomer's suggestions for more flexibility short shrift.

Clearly, the opposition between on the one hand the whimsical narrator and his adventurous reader and on the other the forces of custom and orderly functioning goes beyond the question of literary innovation. Narrator and reader are exemplary instances of those who accept the expressionist's notion of the world. They understand that in a paradoxical world there can be "brillantes primeras equivocaciones,"[80] as the newcomer characterizes his literary efforts. Unlike believers in a well-ordered universe, they do not insist upon writings "que tuvieran la solución cerca, y, además, que ocuparan un solo lugar."[81] The narrator counts on a reader who can recognize the value of things half-glimpsed and intuited. He expects the reader to share his own view of the world: "En aquel tiempo yo era socialista y materialista. Hoy soy anarquista spenceriano y místico. Es cierto que entonces mi poder era mucho mayor que hoy, pero es cierto por otra parte que hoy mi sensibilidad, mi contenido psicológico cotidiano es mucho más pobre y por tanto mucho más fácil de estudiar en su misterio, en su calidad metafísica, pues todo estado sentido, por insignificante en duración o intensidad que sea, representa la totalidad del interrogante metafísico." [82]

VI

What, however, of those readers who resist the narrator's camaraderie, his continual suggestions that narrator and reader share a privileged and superior view of the universe? What of those who continue to believe that a work of literature ought to be read from beginning to end, in a rigorous and systematic fashion? Just as erratic, imaginative readers find encouragement both in the narrator's remarks and in the structure of his work, systematic readers find discouragement and disapproval. Macedonio's works are designed to reward readers who share his approach and to give great difficulty to those who resist his notions about reading and writing.

Perhaps the most open manifestation is the scolding addressed to linear readers in *Museo de la novela de la Eterna*. As mentioned above, the narrator attempts to win these remiss souls over to a more flexible reading, suggesting that they adopt a less rigid view of time and existence as well. This individual otherwise has an effect on the novel that he reads in such an uncongenial manner: "arruinaría y delataría todo mi escamoteo de autor débil y recursista fiado en que se salvarían todos sus incompleteces, inadvertidas." [83] With his antagonistic reading, he also "betrays" the fragmentary, ambiguous characters. This stodgy reader could especially use the lessons to be learned from an appropriate reading of the work: "ojalá te corrija de tu bilis de publicador de defectos." [84]

Such a reader, however, will find it very difficult to carry out a reading at cross-purposes with the writing itself. Among the features which frustrate such a reading the most obvious is the fragmentation found in all Macedonian writings. As the narrator once remarks, there can be no really systematic reader of *Museo de la novela de la Eterna,* since even "el lector seguido tendrá la sensación de una nueva manera de saltear: la de seguir al autor que salta." [85] The interconnections between chapter and chapter or even paragraph and paragraph are notably tenuous.

For instance, in the "Confesiones de un recienvenido al mundo literario (esforzados estudios y brillantes primeras equivocaciones)" the newcomer attempts a self-definition. After discussing merchandizing, insomnia, authenticity and other matters, the newcomer begins the formulation of the definition. He says that a newcomer is one who does not know how to resemble those around him because he has not learned their customs and expectations: "no sabe si se ha puesto los pantalones al revés, o el sombrero derecho en la cabeza izquierda." [86] The only defense of the newcomer in such an anomalous situation is this: "se concentra en una meditación sobre eclipses, ceguera de los transeúntes, huelga de los repartidores de luz, invisibilidad de los átomos y del dinero de papá, y así logra no ser visto." [87] While this definition may appear to have strayed from the theme announced by the title of

this rambling note, it does comment on what the literary
newcomer is attempting. Rather than observe and master the
norms of those around him, who constitute "la clase de los
diferentes,"[88] the newcomer looks to his own notions. His
idea of what is most worth having in a literary work does
not include unity and coherence, and readers demanding those
features cannot read him.

Another feature designed to frustrate the too-linear
reader is the enormous amount of redundancy in Macedonio's
writings. Frequent restatements of the same ideas occur:
that the best state of consciousness is one combining elements of sleep and waking, that man ought not to order his
life according to standards imposed from without and that
rational inquiry has its limits. Macedonio himself comments
on his repetitions when he wishes to give young people "la
exposición mas cuidadosa y completa posible de la verdad
y necesidad de la actitud mística. También la beldad
cívica, o sea la Libertad, el Estado Mínimo, que es mi
otro tema u obsesión, será otro de mis tópicos."[89] Needless
to say, a high occurrence of repetition can quickly cause
an otherwise linear reader to become the Macedonian ideal
lector salteado.

A third structural impediment to a reassuringly "complete" reading is one found also in Arlt's Erdosain novels:
the ending that fails to give a sense of closure. The last
of the several commentaries following the *Museo de la
novela de la Eterna* states: "Lo dejo libro abierto: será
acaso el primer 'libro abierto' en la historia literaria...."[90] Like the Archpriest of Hita in his famous
invitation to readers of the *Libro de buen amor,* the *Museo*
narrator asks readers to modify the text in accord with
their own esthetic needs and impulses. He "deja autori-
zado a todo escritor futuro de impulso y circunstancias
que favorezcan un intenso trabajo, para corregirlo y
editarlo libremente, con o sin mención de mi nombre...
Suprima, enmiende, cambie, pero, si acaso, que algo
quede."[91]

Museo de la novela de la Eterna is also open in a
second, less easily comprehensible way. After inviting
reader collaboration, the narrator confesses that his work
as it stands "está muy lejos de la fórmula de la belarte
de personajes por la palabra,"[92] an ideal of writing that
he has expounded throughout the work. The literary theory
scattered throughout the *Museo de la novela de la Eterna*
is remarkably difficult to follow, not only because of its
originality, but because of the elliptical, enigmatic
fashion in which it is presented. One coherent system of
principles has been disentangled from the work by Jitrik,
who presents them in programmatic and accessible manner
in his essay "La 'novela futura' de Macedonio Fernández."[93]
However, the reader of the last chapter of the *Museo* is
hard-pressed to find these novelistic principles in the
summary provided: "En esta oportunidad insisto en que la
verdadera ejecución de mi teroría novelística sólo podría
cumplirse escribiendo la novela de varias personas que se
juntan para leer otra, de manera que ellas, lectores-
personajes, lectores de la otra novela personajes de ésta,
se perfilaran incesantemente como personajes existentes,
no 'personajes,' por contrachoque con las figuras e imágenes
de la novela por ellos mismos leída."[94]

Thus, the reader comes to the last chapter only to discover that the real work of achieving the writing still lies ahead: "Queda también esto, pues, como 'empresa abierta.'"[95] What he has read, although it looks like the work itself, is only "una imperfecta pieza de ejecución"[96] of the desired novel. Moreover, his efforts are required to bring this ideal novel into existence, although what he must do remains altogether unclear. Unless he is reading with, for example, Jitrik's guide to Macedonio's novelistic notions in hand, the reader is unlikely to have a clear notion of the ideal novel that he is to bring into existence.

Again, the narrator reassures those readers who can accept confusion, ambiguity and a garbled presentation of important matters. "Este confusionismo deliberado es probablemente de una fecundidad conciencial liberadora; labor de genuina artisticidad; artificiosidad fecunda para la conciencia en su efecto de fragilizar la noción y certeza de ser," he says,[97] in an altogether expressionistic statement of principles. To deal with a world that cannot be grasped through rational inquiry and thorough reflection over observable phenomena, man should have a literature that will force him to develop a more intuitive, "mystical" approach. In this spirit, Macedonio calls one writing "La oratoria de un hombre confuso."[98] He proclaims his confused condition because it is a more salutary one than addiction to fallacious certainties. On another occasion, he explains the purpose of his words: "Os dejo contaminados con estos problemas de que adolezco"[99] rather than supply conclusions in a world notably lacking in tidy conclusions.

Thus, in Macedonio Fernández as in Arlt, structural aspects of the work reinforce the thematic statements made therein. The writing speaks of how man is to deal with a universe resistant to purely rational inquiry and often unintelligible to man. At the same time, it confronts the reader with elements that cannot be altogether understood and whose sense may escape the reader altogether. What one must do to accommodate himself to the writing is homologous to what he must do to live in an illogical world.

The narrative voice in all Macedonio's writings is important in persuading the reader to accept the irrational, the irregular and the arbitrary. This narrator makes some powerful assumptions. He presupposes that most readers will be receptive to his innovations: "la gente seguía leyendo malo--lo que tengo que agradecer a sus malos autores--y esperando bueno."[100] Giving the reader every benefit of the doubt, the narrator of *Museo de la novela de la Eterna* assumes that none or perhaps one of his readers will be so insensitive as to pursue a linear reading, and even that one may yet be redeemed.

The narrator expresses praise for and solidarity with the reader who accepts the writing on its own erratic terms, not attempting to force it into preexisting modes. He makes the reader his confederate and colleague, for without the reader's cooperation the good novel will never be a reality: "construyamos una novela así que por una buena vez no sea clara, fiel copia realista."[101] As the writer struggles against the dead weight of the past, the reader is his ally and

confidant. It is continually presupposed that the reader
will side with the innovative novelist against those who
seek to place constraints on his writing. In turn, the
novelist will help rescue readers from the wasteland of
extant literature: "que siguieran leyendo indulgentes la
mala (novela) aliviados por la conciencia de que ya la
buena venía, pues sé que es virtud de lectores dedicados
esperar leyendo." [102] The current state of literature is
not the fault of readers, but rather of editors, official
literati and the difficulty of creating the heralded new
novel: "siendo muy buena la nueva novelística, no se
sabe todavía cuándo la habrá." [103]

Readers who fall short of these optimistic expectations must struggle against structural impediments designed to frustrate their attempts at systematic reading.
Even should an obstinate reader pursue every page in con-
secutive order, he will find the narrator skipping around
in order to prevent a linear reading.

Fragmentation, a staggering amount of redundancy and
the lack of closure all militate against a conventional
reading. *Museo de la novela de la Eterna,* for instance,
opens with over a hundred pages of prologues and introductions. In the face of such massive repetition, even systematic readers may become Macedonio's ideal *lectores
salteados.* Nor can one assume upon finishing the last
page that he "has read" the work. Emendations, inter-
calations, additional material and even the omission of
parts of the work are invited. The attempt to make a good
novel, moreover, is not only the work of the author, but
requires the participation of the reader. However, the
reader is not told in so many words what his part in this
undertaking must be. Rather he is given a cryptic, sphinx-
like summary of the main tenets of Macedonio's great novelistic scheme, along with a reminder that confusion is a
productive state of mind. To the *lector seguido,* anxious
for linearity and conclusions, such an ending is difficult
to bear. Again, the dichotomy is established between those
who need to impose cosmos on chaos through rational means
and the self-proclaimed *hombre confuso* who can confront
the disorderly and the irrational honestly.

As in all the expressionistic works discussed so far,
a strong case is made for the necessity of developing nonrational approaches to reality as the rational ones prove
unsatisfactory. Arlt's Astrologer makes this point over
and over in his speeches: a totally rationalistic way of
looking at the world is unsatisfactory for man. The
Astrologer predicates all his actions on the existence of
strong irrational forces, rather than on the inherent order
of the universe and the rationality of his fellow men. He
is the character most able to achieve what he sets out to
do precisely because he does not rely on a falsely ordered
notion of the world.

Similarly, Macedonio's writings refute the notion
that one can learn about the universe by the application
of reason. Instead, "la mística" must be the faculty cultivated by man in order to acquire the knowledge most worth
having. [104] These and other strongly antirationalistic
statements find their counterpart in the wildly disordered

narrative of the expressionists.   This disheveled mode of presentation serves a function: that of making the reader renounce his addiction to order and system in favor of an orientation more appropriate to the world in which he must live.

ENDNOTES

1. *Menschheitsdämmerung: Symphonie jungster Dichtung,* ed. Kurt Pinthus (Berlin: Rohwolt, 1920).

2. Kurt Pinthus, introduction to *Menschheitsdämmerung,* trans. Henry Hatfield in his *Modern German Literature* (New York: St. Martin's Press, 1967), p. 60.

3. Pinthus, trans. in Hatfield, p. 60.

4. Pinthus, trans. in Hatfield, p. 60.

5. Derek van Abbé, *Image of a People* (New York: Barnes and Noble, 1964), p. 136.

6. Richard Samuel, and R. Hinton Thomas, *Expressionism in German Life, Literature and the Theatre* (Philadelphia: Albert Saifer, 1971), p. 45.

7. van Abbé, p. 137.

8. Ibid.

9. Wolfgang Kayser, *Interpretación y análisis de la obra literaria;* 4. ed. rev. (Madrid: Gredos, 1964), p. 230.

10. Kayser, p. 230.

11. Walter H. Sokel, *The Writer in Extremis: Expressionism in Twentieth-Century German Literature* (Stanford: Stanford University Press, 1959), p. 62.

12. Sokel, p. 68.

13. Hatfield, p. 73.

14. Hatfield, pp. 72-73.

15. van Abbé, p. 136.

16. van Abbé, p. 136.

17. Hatfield, pp. 64-65.

18. Kayser, p. 193.

19. See Guillermo de Torre, "Para la prehistoria ultraísta de Borges," *Hispania,* 47 (1964), 457-63.

20. van Abbé, p. 133.

21. van Abbé, p. 135.

22. For example, such a reevaluation is made by David Viñas, "El escritor vacilante: Arlt, Boedo y Discépolo," in his *Literatura argentina y realidad política, de Sarmiento a Cortázar* (Buenos Aires: Siglo Veinte, 1971), pp. 67-73.

23. A point argued by Eduardo González Lanuza in his
    Roberto Arlt (Buenos Aires: Centro Editor, 1971),
    pp. 88-89.

24. Roberto Arlt, *Los siete locos* (Buenos Aires: Losada,
    1968), p. 140.

25. Roberto Arlt, "El traje del fantasma," in his *El
    jorobadito* (Buenos Aires: Fabril, 1968), p. 187.

26. Arlt, *Los siete locos*, p. 102.

27. Arlt, *Los siete locos*, p. 119.

28. Arlt, *Los siete locos*, p. 198.

29. Arlt, *Los siete locos*, p. 137.

30. Nathalie Sarraute, *L'Ere du soupçon: essais sur le
    roman* (Paris: Gallimard, 1956).

31. Alberto Vanasco, introductory essay to Roberto Arlt,
    Regreso (Buenos Aires: Corregidor, 1972), p. 13.

32. Arlt, *Los lanzallamas* (Buenos Aires: Fabril, 1968),
    p. 89.

33. Arlt, *Los lanzallamas*, p. 299.

34. Ibid.

35. Arlt, *Los siete locos*, p. 42.

36. Arlt, *Los siete locos*, p. 122.

37. Arlt, *Los lanzallamas*, p. 75.

38. Arlt, *Los siete locos*, p. 34.

39. Arlt, *Los siete locos*, p. 77.

40. Arlt, *Los siete locos*, p. 65.

41. Arlt, *Los siete locos*, p. 34.

42. Mirta Arlt, preface to Arlt, *Los siete locos*, p. i.

43. Stasys Gostautas, "La evasión de la ciudad en las
    novelas de Roberto Arlt," *Revista iberoamericana*,
    No. 80 (1972), 441-62.

44. Arlt, *Los lanzallamas*, pp. 22-23.

45. Albert Vanasco, pp. 9-21.

46. Arlt, *Los siete locos*, p. 33.

47. Arlt, introduction to his *Los lanzallamas*, p. 12.

48. Arlt, introduction to his *Los lanzallamas,* p. 11.

49. Arlt, dedication to *El jorobadito,* p. 18.

50. Ibid.

51. Arlt, *El criador de gorilas* (Buenos Aires: Editorial Universitaria, 1964), p. 13.

52. Carmelina de Castellanos, for instance, makes this comment in her *Tres nombres en la novela argentina* (Santa Fe: Editorial Colmegna, 1962), p. 35, as does Eduardo González Lanuza, p. 77.

53. Arlt, cited in Adolfo Prieto's introductory essay to *Un relato inédito de Roberto Arlt* (Buenos Aires: Editorial Contemporánea, 1968), p. 19.

54. Arlt, *Los lanzallamas,* p. 15.

55. For instance, González Lanuza finds it a puerile trick; see p. 88.

56. Adolfo de Obieta, introduction to Macedonio Fernández, *Papeles de recienvenido* (Buenos Aires: Centro Editor, 1966), p. 5.

57. Noé Jitrik, "La 'novela futura' de Macedonio Fernández," in *Nueva novela latinoamericana,* ed. Jorge Lafforgue (Buenos Aires: Paidós, 1969-72), II, 34.

58. Jitrik, "La 'novela futura'," pp. 34-35.

59. Jitrik, "La 'novela futura'," p. 30.

60. Noé Jitrik, "Bipolaridad en la historia de la literatura argentina," in his *Ensayos y estudios de literatura argentina* (Buenos Aires: Galerna, 1970), p. 239.

61. Jean Franco, *The Modern Culture of Latin America;* rev. ed. (Middlesex, England: 1970), p. 206.

62. Germán L. García, *Macedonio Fernández: la escritura en objeto* (Buenos Aires: Siglo Veinte, 1975), p. 12.

63. Jitrik, "La 'novela futura' de Macedonio Fernández," p. 30.

64. Macedonio Fernández, *Papeles de recienvenido,* p. 35.

65. Fernández, *Papeles de recienvenido,* p. 42.

66. Fernández, *Papeles de recienvenido,* p. 41.

67. Fernández, *Museo de la novela de la Eterna* (Buenos Aires: Centro Editor, 1967), p. 111.

68. Fernández, *Museo de la novela de la Eterna,* p. 112.

69. Fernández, *Museo de la novela de la Eterna*, p. 111.

70. Fernández, *Museo de la novela de la Eterna*, p. 112.

71. García, p. 28.

72. Fernández, *Papeles de recienvenido*, p. 41.

73. Fernández, *Papeles de recienvenido*, p. 41.

74. Fernández, *Museo de la novela de la Eterna*, p. 111.

75. Ibid.

76. Ibid.

77. Fernández, *Museo de la novela de la Eterna*, p. 112.

78. Fernández, *Papeles de recienvenido*, p. 42.

79. Fernández, *Papeles de recienvenido*, p. 42.

80. Fernández, *Papeles de recienvenido*, p. 35.

81. Fernández, *Papeles de recienvenido*, p. 42.

82. Fernández, *Papeles de recienvenido*, p. 54.

83. Fernández, *Museo de la novela de la Eterna*, p. 112.

84. Ibid.

85. Ibid.

86. Fernández, *Papeles de recienvenido*, p. 36.

87. Ibid.

88. Ibid.

89. Fernández, *Papeles de recienvenido*, p. 55.

90. Fernández, *Museo de la novela de la Eterna*, p. 236.

91. Ibid.

92. Ibid.

93. Noé Jitrik, "La 'novela futura' de Macedonio Fernández," pp. 30-70.

94. Fernández, *Museo de la novela de la Eterna*, p. 236.

95. Ibid.

96. Ibid.

97. Fernández, *Museo de la novela de la Eterna*, p. 237.

98. Fernández, *Papeles de recienvenido*, p. 60.

99. Fernández, *Papeles de recienvenido*, p. 59.

100. Fernández, *Museo de la novela de la Eterna*, pp. 108-109.

101. Fernández, *Museo de la novela de la Eterna*, p. 109.

102. Fernández, *Museo de la novela de la Eterna*, p. 108.

103. Fernández, *Museo de la novela de la Eterna*, p. 109.

104. Fernández, *Papeles de recienvenido*, pp. 54-55.

Chapter 4

The Character in Expressionistic Fiction

The expressionists' deviance from the tenets of realism and naturalism can nowhere be more clearly seen than
in the fictional representation of human figures. The
expressionist rejects the notion that a fictional character ought to resemble real-life human beings in a direct
and immediately perceptible way. The characters in an
expressionistic work stand in some relation to the persons
one encounters in reality, for they serve to comment on
existence as experienced by real-life men. However, this
relation may be a highly metaphorical one, not easily
comprehended even by the reader willing to abandon verisimilitude. As one critic put it, the expressionist bypasses
the accurate representation of surfaces in favor of what
"lies hidden below the more or less placid surface of the
'realist' man, but [is] nevertheless a motivating force of
his inner being and thus much more important than his social
character."[1] Walter H. Sokel characterized the expressionistic representation of human beings as a process of distortion, a process performed in the belief that "distortion
reveals essence."[2] The character resulting from this de-
formation presents the reader with a special set of problems.
He can no longer assume that the character can be measured
against non-literary reality. The expressionistic fictional
universe is an exaggerated, extreme place, and the character's attitudes and behavior must be seen within that
context. The character's wildly aberrant features may be
an oblique comment on some aspect of our own reality that
we do not ordinarily consider bizarre or grotesque. In
fact, the distortion may serve precisely to make manifest
the curious behavior that civilized man is taught to accept
as the norm.

The works of German expressionism are rife with characters whose very existence is an affront to the realist
requirement of verisimilitude. For instance, a commentator
finds early expressionistic tendencies in Franz Wedekind's
"mastery of the grotesque, his bold portrayal of
extreme characters--archetypes or caricatures."[3] The playwright's 1895 *Erdgeist* has as its heroine a savage young
woman who first appears as a dangerous serpent exhibited
in a traveling circus. In the course of the play, the
earth-spirit attracts and kills a number of lovers, each
of whom perceives her differently and calls her by a different name. Hardly a member of the audience could fail
to note that the earth spirit is unlike anything a real-
life woman might be; rather she is an expressionistically
portrayed manifestation of the eternal feminine.

The distortion of the expressionistic character may
manifest itself in extreme forms of behavior, physical
features not found in real-life men, statements revealing
drastic and startling attitudes and linguistic aberrations.
The most celebrated instance of this break with verisi-

militude is the transformation of a clerk into a beetle in
Franz Kafka's 1916 *Die Verwandlung*. In Franz
Wedekind's 1891 *Frühlings Erwachsen,* the hero does not dis-
appear after his suicide, but rather returns to the stage,
his head under his arm as a sign of his alteration. Robert
Wiene's 1919 *Das Cabinet des Dr. Caligari* shows a man so
subjugated by Caligari that he must lie dormant in a box,
emerging to excite paying spectators or murder when willed
to do so by his mentor. Such anomalous conditions stand
in some relation to conditions that afflict mankind in the
real world; it is the task of the reader or audience to
deduce or intuit what the relation might be. One has only
to think of the critical discussions on why Kafka's clerk
should become a beetle to see what importance that task
may assume. We cannot consider such expressionistic characters without first recognizing and considering their
deviance from real-life notions of what a human being is
like. As Wolfgang Kayser points out, even the most bizarre
features of expressionism must be discussed not as mere
curiosities or defects, but as part of the expressionists'
attempt to convey a certain view of existence, literature
and language. Readers must try to see the function of the
most extravagantly distorted and garbled modes of representation.[4] Walter H. Stokel also would remind readers to
view the non-verisimilar fictional world of expressionism as
an attempt to confront them with the most essential truths.[5]

Arlt's novels, for instance, present characters to the
reader in a most irregular fashion. One is puzzled both by
the lavishness and by the chariness of narrative data.
Often the most minute details are given to the reader,
while major problems are left uncommented on. For instance,
we are told several times that Erdosain stole exactly
$600.07, but not whether he is a good enough inventor to
realize his grandiose plans. Erdosain's great ambition
and technological schemes are important to the plot of the
two Erdosain novels, while the $600.07 is hardly important
at all. When one of Erdosain's fellow conspirators,
Haffner, is dying, we learn many details of his shabby
past. However, we do not find out why his former cohorts
have decided to assassinate him. As for the group's chief
ideologist, the Astrologer, it is never made clear what
ideology he is espousing from page to page. Nor is it
known whether he had any real revolution planned or whether
he formed the conspiracy as part of some elaborate joke.
Many personal anecdotes about members are disclosed, often
at moments when they seem least germane. The reader finds
himself knowing many things about the characters that he
does not need to know and having to imagine the points he
most likely wants to know.

One area within the confused mass of Arltian data that
might be further examined is that of physical descriptions
of characters. Characters are only occasionally described
as wholes, programmatically or feature by feature. Rather,
bits of information about their physical characteristics
come out from time to time, seemingly at random. Moreover,
there is a good deal of repetition. We are told an amazing
number of times that the Astrologer has a rhomboid-shaped
face, that Hipólita has red hair and that Barsut is forever
watching the same corner of any room he occupies. But we

do not learn until the second of the two novels is nearly over how small and feeble-appearing Erdosain really is.

The first noticeable pattern in the physical aspects of the characters is that so many have greater or lesser deformities. La Bizca, La Cieguita and El Jorobadito figure among the Arlt characters metonymically named for some highly visible and unfortunate anomaly. Next to them are characters who have a less grotesque or obvious oddity. The Astrologer is castrated and has a face in the shape of a rhombus. Hipólita has red hair, often something of a sign of marginality. Erdosain has a habit of turning pale that is outside his control and often untimely, since it causes people to stop and wonder over him. One critic found Erdosain's pallors a sign of undisguisable guilt.[6]

Other physical characteristics are not odd in themselves but rather inappropriate in context. Erdosain's preoccupied gaze and pallor upset other passengers on the train he takes at the end of the novel. He is in too dramatic a state for a mere commuter; in fact, he is working up to suicide. A woman, perceiving his state, imagines him to be ill. Later his small size and meek aspect prove ironic. The police have finally caught up with him and expect a great brute: "La sorpresa de la policía al constatar que aquel joven delicado y pálido era 'el feroz asesino Erdosain' no es para ser descripta."[7]

Hipólita's thinness comes up in the same way. She is recalling a stay in the country with a lover. Clearly she did not strike the rustics as a mistress with whom one would escape to the country. While for them the paramour ought to have an opulent figure and an air of luxury, she was only "una mujer delgadita que no tenía dinero, sino pobreza."[8] It seems to them that her lover should have chosen a woman of less poverty-stricken mien.

Finally, there are physical details that happen to catch someone's attention. When Hipólita has her first encounter with the Astrologer and finds herself on the losing end of a battle of wills, she comforts herself with the thought that "Sin duda alguna, mis piernas están bien formadas."[9] Later when she is succumbing to his ideology, she lies in bed trying to summon up her identity as a woman free to make choices. "Yo, yo, Hipólita. Con mi cuerpo, que tiene tres pecas, una en el brazo, otra en la espalda, otra bajo el seno derecho."[10] Certainly knowing the location of Hipólita's body spots does nothing for the reader's comprehension of the plot. Rather it is of interest that Hipólita should be so aware of her body as an integral part of her identity.

In all these examples, the piece of a person that is described is the one that calls attention to itself. Sometimes it is a deformity, sometimes merely an incongruity in a given context. Sometimes it is a relatively normal characteristic which for some reason surges into a character's consciousness. In any case, the whole person, both in his odd and his standard aspects, seldom appears. The point is that in a hypersubjective world, one only really has a trait when attention becomes focused upon it.

II

The temptation to disregard the purposes that underlie the distorted representation of characters in expressionism is only one problem for readers and critics. Equally important is to remember that the expressionistic character inhabits a fictional context purposely constructed to resemble this world only in a figurative, oblique fashion. The relation between the expressionistic fictional world and the real world on which it comments may be so blatantly metaphorical or so puzzling to the reader that he cannot measure it against his own reality. This is certainly the case in, for example, Macedonio Fernández's *Museo de la novela de la Eterna* when a character incinerates himself by carrying a lit candle all the way across Buenos Aires, totally absorbed in his duties as character.[11] Few if any readers would try to classify such behavior using the terms we employ for real-life instances of self-destruction, absent-mindedness or utter dedication to one's work.

However, when elements of distortion and fantastic features exist in the work in more subtle forms, the reader may attempt to impose real-world judgments on characters inhabiting quite another reality. This is certainly a problem for critics of Arlt, an author who, as Adolfo Prieto says, "alimentaba una fuerte tendencia a manifestarse con fórmulas en las que la fantasía juega alucinantes contrapuntos con la experiencia de lo real."[12] Because Arlt's fiction seems at some points close to a documentary realism, one can easily begin to hold his characters to the same standards one uses for individuals in real life and characters in realistic fiction. Why this may not be appropriate is seen in the problem of madness in Arlt's fiction.

It would be difficult to deny that the Arltian characters are given to some very odd behavior. In the two Erdosain novels alone, there is an attempt to poison Buenos Aires with a noxious gas; an inventor of the copper rose and dogs that come in all shades, both supposedly boons to mankind; a revolutionary leader whose models are Lenin, Mussolini, the Ku Klux Klan and the Apocalypse; and a man who expounds a metaphysics of pimping. It is common to conclude that psychoses or at least severe neuroses underlie such curious behavior.

For instance, David Maldavsky, in *Las crisis en la narrativa de Roberto Arlt,* discusses the characters in terms of clinical psychology and finds them to be suffering from Oedipal complexes and other unfortunate conditions found among real-life mental patients. However, the main objection we would make to the view of Arlt represented by Maldavsky's work is precisely that it does insist on comparing Arltian characters to real-life madmen.

The problem is that while real madmen are adjudged to be so because of the way in which they deal with the real world, Arlt's characters must cope with the Arltian world, which is quite a different place. It is so different, in our view, as to impel its inhabitants to the use of strategems which, although neurotic for this world, are necessary to survive in the disordered Arltian world. In other words, we would argue that a good deal of the madness in Arlt is adaptive and serves to make more bearable the existence of the characters.

One main example of what strikes readers as crazy in Arlt are the speeches made by the Astrologer to the conspirators he has recruited. It is impossible to situate the Astrologer ideologically or to follow the thread of his discourse for very long at a time. He himself says, when he has been compared to Lenin, "pero Lenín sabía adónde iba,"[13] implying that he, the Astrologer, has no idea where he is headed. Maldavsky remarks on the odd contrast between the garbled pronouncements of the Astrologer and the willingness of the conspirators to trust in him as an example of the "valores distorsionados" endemic in Arlt's fiction.[14]

Certain arguments can be made for the relative validity of the Astrologer's words. One is that none of the consistent sorts of thinking found in Arlt seems to work at all. For instance, Elsa, Erdosain's wife, is an exponent of holding down a job, observing societal norms and not attempting to reorder things. One critic who disapproved of her said: "¿Cuáles son los mecanismos que, según Arlt, a través de las que la sociedad burguesa lleva a cabo la aniquilación del individuo? El más importante de todos se efectúa a través de la mujer, en este caso Elsa, la típica burguesita."[15]

Elsa's ideas are consistent and predictable but offer her little help in dealing with all the chaotic happenings in the novel. The same thing could be said for the police, who are remarkably inept in their pursuit of the conspirators. They only find Erdosain after he has facilitated their task by committing suicide on a commuter train. Even then, they can hardly believe that it is he; he is too meek-looking to be "el feroz asesino Erdosain,"[16] object of a massive manhunt. The consistent, sane beliefs held by the police are useful only so long as reality behaves according to "sane" expectations. Murderers ought to look malicious and conspirators ought to operate in a more organized way than do the Astrologer's men. Thus, thinking about reality in a consistent manner can be a handicap if the universe is constantly presenting aberrations.

Several things about the Astrologer suggest that he has adopted an other-than-rational mode of dealing with an irregular world and may not even be attempting rationalism. One is his profession, that of astrologer; he also demonstrates upon occasion a certain proficiency at Apocalyptic exegesis. Occultists, of course, have a tradition of veiling what they say so as not to run the risks of communication with noninitiates. Moreover, they are situated within an antirationalist tradition that seeks to circumvent the institutionalized ways of dealing with reality. The Astrologer works from within this tradition of subterfuge. He fakes the murder of Barsut and lets Erdosain believe himself to be responsible for this nonexistent murder. He introduces a friend of his as a major to the conspirators only to reveal him as a fraud soon after, thus providing an object lesson in the superiority of appearances over reality. A footnote tells the reader that the Major was real and the revelation of his imposture was a lie. Erdosain finds it very hard to extract from any of the conspirators what they really think about the feasibility of the Astrologer's projected revolution. All this suggests that the

Astrologer and his friends are covertly but purposefully
using confusion to plan something that only superficially
resembles a real-life revolution. As David Viñas puts it,
they are "siete magos" whose recourse is "la mirada que
seduce" rather than banal logistics.[17]
     In other writings, Arlt has commented on the privi-
lege enjoyed by occultists of bypassing rational forms of
communication. In one journalistic piece he says that oc-
cult powers are innate and occur in persons totally unable
to verbalize about their faculties or to carry them over
into spiritual grandeur: "No son personas de extraordinaria
cultura ni de vida interior semejante a la de Buda o de
Cristo."[18] In another journalistic note, an occultist is
described as talking nonsense, just as the Astrologer does
at times. Arlt is willing to accept the adept's explanation, which is that the nonsense speech serves to establish
propitious vibrations phonetically rather than to convey
meaning conventionally. Since occultists are not obliged
to tell non-occultists what they are doing nor to proceed
in rational fashion, it is possible that the garbled pronouncements of the Astrologer work rather well as communication among his intimates and that the reader, a non-
initiate, is being excluded.
     Much of the same principle seems to hold for Erdo-
sain's career as an inventor, which makes no sense on a
literal level. It is clear to the reader that Erdosain
has not the resources to carry out his plans, which in any
event seem crazy inventions: a copper rose, that is to
say, a rose divested of all its appealingly roselike features, and a machine to poison Buenos Aires with gas. The
harsh metallic rose elicits the admiration of nearly everyone except Hipólita, who voices her objection only near
the end of Los siete locos.
     Before Hipólita's objection, the Astrologer and his
men had admired the rose scheme, Erdosain's wife had stopped
in the midst of abandoning him while she and her new man
admired the idea and a whole family, the Espilas, seemed
to exist only to admire Erdosain's genius as inventor.
Again it seems likely that these characters understand some
alchemical, nonliteral virtue in the transformation of a
rose to copper that has nothing to do with how DuPont, say,
would consider a proposed invention. The reader, again, is
excluded from some special understanding among the characters and sees no reason to turn fresh, soft, fragrant
roses into hard, metallic objects.
     The poisonous gasworks are not a rational way of
dealing with urban problems or with problems of any other
sort. Yet, the characters to whom Erdosain explains the
plan are able to seize immediately on the kind of gratifi-
cation that its implementation might bring. "Quiero per-
mitirme el lujo de ver caer a la gente, por la calle, como
caen las langostas," says the Astrologer.[19] It would be
hard to paraphrase the exact meaning of the gasworks, but
even the uninitiated reader can see that it serves some
function of catharsis for the rancor of the characters and
purgation for the city, like a Biblical scourge.
     On a more personal level, too, the characters in Arlt
have developed irrational ways of coping with their exist-
ences. Erdosain, for instance, has a completely developed

set of fantasies with which to provide himself relief from his anguish. In them, a wealthy eccentric is magnetically drawn to Erdosain and impelled to solve all the unhappy man's financial, spiritual and emotional difficulties. Erdosain eases his bad moments by willfully blurring the separation between reality and fantasy until his benefactor seems to be in his immediate area, waiting to be pulled in by Erdosain's irresistible aura.

Erdosain is also able to obtain release by the formulation of an essentially nonsense sentence: "No me importa. Dios se aburre igual que el Diablo." The only meaning to this utterance is that it constitutes a barrage of irrationality aimed at the massive unfairness of life. It works, though: "Le causó alegria el pensamiento, estaba contento de su ocurrencia."[20]

The classification, measurement and examination of his own unhappiness has become habitual with Erdosain, and he apparently finds this procedure more bearable than mere passive suffering. He invents metaphors for his discontent that Arltian critics have often remarked upon for their innovative nature. Chapters in the Erdosain novels are entitled "Círculo de angustia" and "Cortina de angustia." Erdosain also ponders at length the sources of his distress, weighs its metaphysical importance and explains his erratic behavior thus: "Uno roba, hace macanas porque está angustiado."[21]

For what reason do the characters in Arlt construct such elaborate systems of irrational behavior? The main one is in order to survive in the expressionist universe, a garbled world where normal behavior is of little avail. The normal behavior of Elsa and the police certainly bring them no advantage; it is the police's belief that things will make sense that renders them unable to recognize Erdosain. The Astrologer, in particular, is frank about his wish to be a survivor. When asked about the possible failure of his plans, he replies: "Entonces los que pagarán serán ustedes, yo no."[22] In fact, it is the Astrologer who survives at the end of the two novels, along with Hipólita, who has subordinated herself to him. Even if the Arltian characters who propose irrational strategems for an irrational world are destroyed, they have more awareness, style and wit in their defeat. Erdosain is marvelously in control of himself when he dies, having choreographed his suicide elaborately. He even remains sitting after having shot himself, which the narrator interprets as a valiant manifestation of decorum. Surviving literally or only metaphorically, such "survivor" characters have a distinct esthetic advantage over those characters who blindly persist in behavior that would be appropriate only to a world where reason still obtained.

Irrationality in Arlt is adaptive for a second, more practical reason. The characters are conspirators, and it is often to their advantage to hide behind a baffling, enigmatic self while they work out their *modus operandi*. Thus they are in the opposite position from most real-life people, who strive to present a consistent and clear-thinking self to others even when they are inwardly too confused to think anything. Erdosain and the Astrologer like to keep others in awe of their nonrational, seductive, unarticulated powers.

Thus besides being suitable to a deranged world, irrationality is a good way to impress those who are still trying to
work logically. Considering the chaotic conditions that
obtain in Arlt's fiction, crazy behavior may be the most
logical sort; at any rate it can hardly be considered the
same sort of madness that afflicts people living in the
real world.

III

Perhaps the difference between the expressionistic
character and the character of documentary realism, who can
be measured against real-world counterparts, can be seen by
examining how one Arlt character deviates from the realist
norm. Hipólita, a character in the Erdosain novels, shows
an especially revealing kind of aberrance since she is a
prostitute. What could be more typical of the attempt to
convey social truths through literature than the creation of
a fictional prostitute who recounts her recruitment and ini-
tiation into the demimonde and her experiences among its
marginal inhabitants? Arlt's Hipólita superficially fits
the pattern but, as we will see, she offers the reader
"truths" that are far from the sociological or psychological
insights represented by the prostitute of realist or naturalist fiction. In fact, the way in which Hipólita is
presented implies a questioning of the very principles of
sociological and psychological inquiry. She makes us doubt
whether human conduct is really governed by a set of dis-
cernible rules which can be discovered by rational means.
A science that looks for uniformities and generalizations
on which it can base its assertions can only study phenomena
that will reveal such uniformities of occurrence. According
to expressionism, the human being is no such predictable
phenomenon; he can only be characterized in ways that
bypass the rational and the scientific.

A celebrated attempt to inform the reader about real-
life prostitutes through a fictional equivalent is Manuel
Gálvez's 1919 *Nacha Regules*. This work accepts the premise
that those who study man comprehend, as a sociology text-
book states, by discovering "uniformities in the many complex phenomena which they study, in order to reduce them
to a smaller number of principles. When such principles
have become precisely stated and sufficiently verified, they
are considered scientific laws."[23]

Nacha Regules commented upon a problem that was causing
widespread concern in Buenos Aires in the early part of this
century. Prostitution and, in particular, the white slave
trade excited concern. Gálvez's 1905 doctoral thesis, *La
trata de blancas,* was an academic investigation, while
Alberto Londres's widely-read *El camino a Buenos Ayres* (1924)
took a journalistic look at the matter.[24] Those who were
outraged by the publication of *Nacha Regules* presupposed a
close interrelationship between real-life prostitution and
its fictional representation. Even Noé Jitrik, who questions
Gálvez's worth as investigator of social forces, recognizes
the realist intentions of the writing: "*Nacha Regules*
primero e *Historia de arrabal* después, fueron presentadas
como novelas cuyo acento principal estaba puesta en la denuncia de un problema social general...."[25] Jitrik admits that

on the surface Gálvez's work approaches the realist goal of
a direct, unmediated transcription of reality: "todas las
novelas de Gálvez se permeabilizan a las exigencias de una
realidad exterior bien determinada y concreta que, en lo
esencial, procede en mínima medida de frecuentaciones liter-
arias."[26]

The prostitute of realist fiction must meet certain
demands or the reader will reject her as inverisimilar.
When Nacha tells her story, the reader must see what happened
to her as typical of the lives of real-life prostitutes:
the factors in her career, the lack of viable job oppor-
tunities for young single women and the influence of the
coercive Pampa Arnedo, who contrives to keep her submerged
in the demimonde. The reader must believe that a woman
may be wooed, bullied and initiated into prostitution by
the strategems the Pampa uses on Nacha. He must accept
that, like Nacha, real women remain prostitutes for lack
of other options. If Nacha's tale is too unlike real-life
occurrences, the reader feels defrauded.

Arlt's Hipólita, on the other hand, does not withstand
measurement against observable reality. Indeed, she is
scarcely measurable against herself, for her characteristics vary in the course of the novels. As an instance of
the erratic manner in which she is presented, let us look
at the extreme differences between her "direct" and her
"indirect" entries into Erdosain's life.

Upon first seeing Hipólita in person, Erdosain is
shocked by her hard coarseness: "me la imaginaba a usted
menos fría...."[27] By means of a flashback, the reader learns
where Erdosain obtained this softer image of Hipólita.
Hipólita's husband offers Erdosain a description in words
and a photograph of Hipólita. Erdosain is understandably
loath to accept the verbal characterization, for the husband
is a mad gambler who finds homologies between the couple's
lives and the Apocalypse. Though Hipólita is a veteran at
her work, he attributes to her an otherworldly quality:
"A momentos me parece que ha bajado de la luna por una
escalera. Donde está ella todos se sentirán felices"
(p. 173).

Erdosain, however, believes the madman's characterization of Hipólita when it is substantiated by a photograph. The filmic image has the ethereal quality Hipólita's
husband attributes to her. The sight of the artless snapshot of Hipólita on a park bench has an immediate effect on
Erdosain: "supo de pronto que junto a Hipólita él no
experimentaría jamás ningún deseo, y esta certidumbre lo
alegró" (p. 168).

A naive-looking snapshot must be the paradigmatic
instance of the attempt to transcribe reality unmediated
by the human imagination: "the camera doesn't lie." But
in the rampantly subjective expressionistic universe of
Arlt's fiction, not even a photographic reproduction is
measurable against observable phenomena. Her husband's
mythmaking has somehow distorted the very process of record-
ing Hipólita on film. Erdosain, who is inordinately fond
of technology and science, believes in the objectivity of
the photograph. He is sure Hipólita must be a "deliciosa
criatura" (p. 173) who has transcended her sordid environment.

Erdosain is profoundly shaken to discover that the photographic representation was just another mythic version of Hipólita, utterly unlike his own firsthand impression of her. He wanders dazedly through Buenos Aires, pondering this contradiction: "¡Qué distinta era la Coja en la realidad! Sin embargo, recordaba lo que le había dicho a Ergueta: -- ¡Qué linda es! ¡Debe tener una gran sensibilidad!" (p. 163). The reader ought not to imagine that Erdosain's relative sanity and Ergueta's overt madness determine their perceptions of Hipólita. Erdosain's view of Hipólita alters substantially in the course of the evening. While his first characterization of her is highly negative, he is later able to say without irony: "ahora no me extraña que Ergueta se haya enamorado de usted. Usted es una mujer admirable" (p. 187).

The shock Erdosain receives upon seeing Hipólita in person is one of many occasioned by his persistent belief that there is one definitive version of all matters. The nature of the expressionistic Arltian universe will not permit such absolute versions. Erdosain frequently questions the other characters to find out if they "really" are making a revolution, extracting gold from mountain lakes, founding a new religion or subverting the Argentine military from within. Inevitably Erdosain's prying meets with equivocal, enigmatic or evasive replies, to his distress. The Astrologer, on the other hand, is a character who can accept a world of exceedingly provisional truths: as Erdosain puts it, "la verdad de la mentira" (p. 148). Hence he is more at home in Arlt's universe, free from the onerous and impossible pursuit of absolute truth. It is significant that while Erdosain kills himself at the end of the novels, the Astrologer, who does not ask life to make sense, survives.

Erdosain's expectations about how life ought to behave are like the expectations of the reader of a sociologically-oriented novel. We see these expectations in the questions with which Erdosain badgers Ergueta. The basis of the marriage eludes him: "¿Pero vos la querés a Hipólita o no?" (p. 173). If it is Biblically ordained, then Ergueta ought not to be concerned with its legal dissolubility: "¿Cómo...todavía no te casaste y ya estás pensando en el divorcio?" (p. 172). Nor can Erdosain reconcile Ergueta's moral regeneration through Biblical exegesis with his continued immersion in Buenos Aires lowlife. Ergueta has no real answers to these questions because they all presuppose the existence of a universe in which things either are or are not true as verifiable by some objective standard. Unless the reader cares to be as confused and frustrated as Erdosain, he must accept the contradictory events of the plot as proper to a world not made up of absolutes.

IV

Besides defying objective assessment, Hipólita breaks with the prostitute of realist fiction by her utter atypicality. Like Nacha Regules, she relates her experiences up to and after entering prostitution. Nacha's story, however, ought to typify what happens to women in real life. The reader may object if any feature of her story is too unrepresentative of prostitutes as a class. Reading Nacha's

story is supposed to inform the reader about the mechanisms
governing commerce in women.

Hipólita, on the other hand, in unapt to furnish sociological insights into prostitution. To begin with, we do
not know how much her story is colored by eagerness to
ingratiate herself with Erdosain, her confidant. The lack
of a reliable narrative voice in the novels makes it impossible to separate "true" memories from touches meant to win
Erdosain's sympathy. The reader is reminded that Hipólita's
story is no more than one version of her life by the discrep-
ancies between her account and Ergueta's. Erdosain recalls
incidents from Hipólita's life as recounted by her husband,
while Hipólita refutes them: " ¿Pero usted cree que estoy
loca!... ¿Por qué iba a regalarle a mi sirvienta un collar
de perlas?" (p. 155). The reader trusts Hipólita more than
her madman-husband, but the divergence between the two
accounts reminds him that all stories mediated by Arltian
characters are highly suspect.

Not only are Hipólita's memories too unreliable to
constitute a case history, they are too atypical. The events
that led her to prostitution are too unlikely to recur in
reality. Unlike Nacha's story, Hipólita's offers no clue
to the phenomenon of prostitution. She was not seduced,
recruited and exploited by a Pampa Arnedo. Nor was prostitution her only way of making a living. In fact, she was
a sheltered maid in a bourgeois household when, on a chaperoned trolley ride, she overheard a discussion of the
profitable "mala vida" (p. 187). Without knowing the meaning of the words, Hipólita awakens to her true vocation
"como si hubiera estado siempre sorda y por primera vez
oyera hablar a la gente" (p. 187). Hipólita's environment,
far from pushing her toward this newly-found vocation, makes
it hard for her to ascertain its nature. Finding those
around her most loath to discuss the matter, Hipólita sends
away for a "manual para ser mujer de mala vida" (p. 188).
The absurd search ends in the office of a lawyer who explains
the essence of prostitution in a polite, yet explicit fashion. It is difficult to abstract from this concatenation
of bizarre events any generalization about how society turns
women into prostitutes.

Nor can we follow the psychic processes that lead
Hipólita to her choice of careers. Like the exterior events
that influence her, her inner workings are anomalous. Two
unlikely-sounding explanations are advanced to account for
her sudden resolve. Hipólita herself offers a quasi-exis-
tential defense of prostitution. She interprets the lawyer's
words: "Por fin dijo: 'En la mujer se llama mala vida los
actos sexuales ejecutados sin amor y para lucrar.' Es decir,
repuse yo, que mediante la mala vida, una se libra del
cuerpo...y queda libre" (p. 188). Erdosain, like the reader,
is puzzled by this explanation. In any event, it would not
explain many real-life instances of prostitution.

Hipólita's reminiscences suggest a second reason for
choosing prostitution: her distress at being the servant-
girl rather than one of the ladies of the house. However,
as she elaborates on this theme, it becomes clear that she
envies respectability as much as wealth. Her fantasies have
a cosily bourgeois coloring. One is a conventional honeymoon
featuring herself as "la recién casada que baja al comedor

en compañía de su esposo hermoso, mientras tintinea la vajilla..." (p. 198). Such an ideal of middle-class wedded bliss could hardly be reached through a career in the demimonde. The reader is again baffled by Hipólita's mental workings. With no reliable narrator on hand to explicate Hipólita's garbled thinking, the reader is again prevented from "learning" about the attitudes and thoughts of prostitutes.

Arlt's Hipólita, then, superficially resembles the prostitute of realist fiction, as exemplified by Nacha Regules. Both characters give a detailed account of their entry into the demiworld, speaking to a male character who is eager to make sense of the matter. However, Nacha's experiences are representative of the societal pressures and psychological processes that make women turn to prostitution in real life. The relationship between Hipólita and any real-life prostitute is, at most, a very indirect and enigmatic one.

The narrator of *Nacha Regules* and Monsalvat, a character knowledgeable on that phenomenon, assure us that prostitution is well represented by Nacha's case history. Since her story is thus important, it is carefully documented for the reader. Hipólita's story, though, is not reliably presented. Indeed, she seems to resist objective presentation: even a snapshot of her reveals more about the two beholders than about the woman depicted. An "objective," reliable characterization of Hipólita cannot come from any of the characters, nor is there a trustworthy central narrator. Unable to ascertain Hipólita's basic characteristics or the "true" story of her life, the reader is frustrated if he attempts to see her as case history.

Nacha's experiences are supposed to be paradigmatic of what happens to real-world prostitutes, and the reader is meant to generalize about the phenomenon of prostitution from Nacha's case. A reader who attempts to read Hipólita's story in search of such generalizations finds himself mocked and frustrated by the eccentricity of her case. Society cannot be blamed for pushing Hipólita toward prostitution or for keeping her in the demiworld. Indeed, she must overcome societal resistance to find out how to enter that world. Few women are drawn to prostitution by prophetic words overhead on a trolley.

If Hipolita's case provides no sociological insights, neither does it supply a composite psychological portrait of the prostitute. The reader knows that Nacha Regules is torn between a desire to escape the demimonde and psychological subjugation to Pampa Arnedo. These two tendencies are supposed to account for much of Nacha's behavior and for the actions of real-world prostitutes as well. Hipólita's psychological workings, though, are inaccessible to the reader. Her existential apology for prostitution baffles the reader and Erdosain both. Nor is her story of class resentment adequate to account for her behavior. Since she envies the bourgeoisie its respectability as much as its wealth, her prostitution is an unlikely means of attaining what she envies. The reader who seeks reasons for Hipólita's actions in her psychological makeup will again meet with frustration. If Hipólita's inner processes do not account for her own behavior, they can hardly explain the behavior of prostitutes as a group.

Arlt's fiction has the trappings of realism: the scabrous details, low-life characters, coarse language and personal accounts of degradation. However, it rejects the realist goal of transcribing real-world phenomena in such a way as to present sociological and psychological insights into their workings. Arlt mocks the reader who expects such "truths" from fiction. Such a reader is frustrated in his attempts to measure Arltian characters against non-literary equivalents or to abstract valid generalizations about social phenomena from the fiction. Erdosain, who wants to think clearly and scientifically about the world around him, experiences just such frustration in the unstable, subjective expressionistic world. He demands to know whether statements and events are true or feigned, possible or unfeasible, but receives no answers to such realist questions. To his horror, even a snapshot proves to be a mythified representation of reality, not a direct and unmediated reproduction. Other characters, most notably the Astrologer, know better than to demand definitive truths from a fluctuating, subjective reality.

Erdosain's fatuous attempts to wrest scientific truths from the chaotic Arltian universe should be a clue to the reader about how to read the novels. If the reader is not to experience Erdosain's frustration, he must abandon the quest for sociological or psychological insights that will be directly applicable to real-world phenomena. He must not expect a definitive version of events and characters or logically acceptable motives for their behavior. Nor can he expect to measure the characters against their real-world equivalents. Rather he must read the work on its own terms, as an antiscientific, imaginative rendering of human existence whose fictional context is the expressionistic Arltian universe.

V

The importance of expressionism as precursor to the *nueva narrativa* can be clearly seen in this bypassing of verisimilitude. The works of the so-called boom years are full of characters whose likeness to real-life persons is distorted, enigmatic and often difficult to grasp. These figurative representations, again, require of the reader that he refrain from measuring fictional characters against the real people he observes in this world. Nor can he assume that these characters illustrate in any direct fashion social and psychological truths, although the novel in which they figure may be making a strong statement about social matters. In many instances, the characters are represented in a way that violates the reader's rational, common-sense notions of how things work. As in the case of the expressionists, the later writers may be trying to force the reader to bypass his rational, "civilized" notions and to read the work with his nonrational faculties engaged.

The number of such characters in contemporary Latin American fiction is enormous. So is the number of ways in which they violate our notions of what is likely or what

makes sense in this world. A vast family of these inverisimilar characters appears in Gabriel García Márquez's 1967
Cien años de soledad, probably the most widely-read of the
boom-year novels. One family member ascends to heaven along
with part of the family wash she was hanging out to dry.
The father, traumatized by the discovery that time leads
nowhere, raves in medieval Latin. A lovesick adolescent
finds solace in eating mud; plagues of insomnia and amnesia
sweep through town; a small-town piano teacher occasions
an outbreak of courtly love. No reader, surely, would
object that insomnia is not among the epidemic diseases or
that courtly love only occurs in a certain cultural context.
There is a good deal of acceptance of such improbable characters as part of the much-discussed "magical realism" typical of so much of the *nueva narrativa*.

Other, less accessible, contemporary works feature
characters whose nature and status are difficult to determine and hence troubling to readers and critics. For instance, Mario Vargas Llosa's 1966 *La casa verde* puzzles one
with this curious ambiguity: Bonifacia and La Selvática may
be two names for one character in view of certain portions
of the text, but in other passages such a definitive identification becomes impossible. In Ernesto Sabato's 1974
Abaddón, el exterminador, a character named Ernesto Sabato
both is and is not the author of the work. While the
Sabato who figures in the plot has written the same works
and incurred the same existential crises as the Sabato whose
name appears on the cover, the former is transformed into a
repellent rodent, while the latter escapes this disgusting
fate. While these unnerving anomalies of character delineation can most acceptably be characterized as magical realism,
they differ from the aberrant presentation of expressionistic
characters only in not falling within the years of expressionism. While expressionism as a movement may have run its
course, its after-effects are massive and widely diffused.

Although the time focus of this study prevents further
discussion of contemporary fictional characters, current
criticism is rife with commentary on this aspect of the
nueva narrativa. The reader of contemporary works must be
continually reconsidering his expectations about literary
characters, their relationship to real-world persons and the
kind of insights they are supposed to offer him. Criticism,
then, must struggle to discover what characters do offer in
the absence of verisimilitude, sociological and psychological
representivity, character development in the recognized sense
and differentiation from other characters in the same work.
For instance, Noé Jitrik, in his *El no existente caballero:
la idea del personaje y su evolución en la narrativa latinoamericana*, says we are witnessing the emergence of a "non-
character."[28] He considers two expressionists, Macedonio
Fernández and the Uruguayan Horacio Quiroga, key figures in
this process. Another critic writes that *La casa verde*
troubles critics because it makes use of the literary character in a way to which they are unaccustomed. He suggests
that a more satisfying reading of the book will result from
rethinking one's preconceived notions about what a literary
character ought to be.[29]

Expressionism, then, challenges the realist notion of
the literary character as a figure who could be compared to

real-life persons in a fairly direct fashion. Instead, the character is meant to resemble real persons only in a metaphorical, often elusive manner. It is especially difficult to consider expressionistic characters apart from the work in which they occur, since their comportment may be improper for the real world but altogether appropriate within the distorted, disordered expressionistic fictional universe. Again, the expressionists give the reader something quite unlike his notions of what literature should offer him. Their characters not only refuse to be compared with real persons but, as in the case of Arlt's Hipólita, are not always comparable to themselves. One character does not always have one stable identity: the Astrologer, for example, renounces the maintenance of a personal identity as an impediment to his work. The very notion of the literary character is disrupted when Macedonio Fernández welcomes all and sundry to be characters in his work, whether they are characters from another text, dedicated readers or simply individuals who chance to see the invitation.

The treatment of literary characters is paradigmatic in two ways of the innovations made by expressionistic literature as a whole. First, literature tells us about reality only in a highly metaphorical fashion, a fashion that the reader must struggle to grasp. The link between real world and fictional world is less accessible and more demanding of the reader's attention than the direct transcription of human realities that was the goal of documentary realism. Secondly, expressionistic literature seeks to disorient the reader by defying what he is apt to consider good sense, order and acceptable literary form. Thus disconcerted, the reader may be forced to abandon his all-too-rational approach to literature and rely on other faculties than reason. He may learn to exercise his intuition, his imagination and all those human capacities that Macedonio Fernández classified as "la mística." [30]

ENDNOTES

1. David William Foster, *Unamuno and the Novel as Expressionistic Conceit* (Hato Rey, P.R.: Inter American University Press, 1973), p. 7.

2. Walter H. Sokel, *The Writer in Extremis: Expressionism in Twentieth-Century German Literature* (Stanford: Stanford University Press, 1959), p. 62.

3. Henry Hatfield, *Modern German Literature* (New York: St. Martin's Press, 1967), p. 64.

4. Wolfgang Kayser, *Interpretación y análisis de la obra literaria*, 4. ed. rev. (Madrid: Gredos, 1966), p. 193, 230.

5. Sokel, pp. 59-62.

6. Alberto Vanasco, introduction to Roberto Arlt, *Regreso* (Buenos Aires: Corregidor, 1972), p. 19.

7. Roberto Arlt, *Los lanzallamas* (Buenos Aires: Fabril, 1968), p. 299.

8. Arlt, *Los lanzallamas*, p. 23.

9. Arlt, *Los lanzallamas*, p. 18.

10. Arlt, *Los lanzallamas*, p. 109.

11. Macedonio Fernández, *Museo de la novela de la Eterna* (Buenos Aires: Centro Editor de América Latina, 1967), p. 22.

12. Adolfo Prieto, introductory essay to Roberto Arlt, *Un relato inédito de Roberto Arlt* (Buenos Aires: Tiempo Contemporáneo, 1968), p. 10.

13. Arlt, *Los lanzallamas*, p. 15.

14. David Maldavsky, *Las crisis en la narrativa de Roberto Arlt* (Buenos Aires: Editorial Escuela, 1968), p. 51.

15. Vanasco, p. 13.

16. Arlt, *Los lanzallamas*, p. 299.

17. David Viñas, *De Sarmiento a Cortázar* (Buenos Aires: Siglo Vientiuno, 1971), p. 69.

18. Arlt, *Aguafuertes porteñas* (Buenos Aires: Losada, 1958), p. 112.

19. Arlt, *Los lanzallamas*, p. 76.

20. Arlt, *Los lanzallamas*, p. 36.

21. Arlt, *Los siete locos* (Buenos Aires: Losada, 1968),
     p. 34.

22. Arlt, *Los lanzallamas*, p. 75.

23. Joseph S. Roucek, and Roland L. Warren, *Sociology:
     An Introduction* (Totowa, N.J.:   Littlefield, Adams and
     Co., 1968), p. 4.

24. Noted by Noé Jitrik in "Los desplazamientos de la culpa
     en las obras 'sociales' de Manuel Gálvez," in his
     Ensayos y estudios de literatura argentina (Buenos
     Aires: Galerna, 1970), p. 58.

25. Ibid.

26. Jitrik, "Los desplazamientos," p. 56.

27. Arlt, *Los siete locos*, p. 173.   Further page numbers
     are from this edition.

28. Noé Jitrik, *El no existente caballero: La idea del
     personaje y su evolución en la narrativa latinoamericana*
     (Buenos Aires: Megápolis, 1975).

29. Michael Moody, "The Web of Defeat: A Thematic View of
     Characterization in Mario Vargas Llosa's *La Casa Verde*,"
     Hispania, 59 (1976), 11-23.

30. Fernández, *Papeles de recienvenido* (Buenos Aires: Centro
     Editor de América Latina, 1966), p. 54.

Chapter 5

Conclusion

I

This study has identified the highly innovative literary works produced by Argentine writers in the years 1915-40 as manifestations of international expressionism. German expressionism, as the most self-proclaimed and widely-recognized flowering of that literary movement, is the model against which one must measure the expressionism of the Argentine authors. Therefore, a discussion of the main tenets of the European movement preceded the commentary on the Latin American writings.

We have tried to show that the most innovative features of the work of Roberto Arlt, Macedonio Fernández, Jorge Luis Borges and Armando Discépolo are essentially the same as the fundamental characteristics of German expressionism. The great fragmentation, purposeful disregard for considerations of verisimilitude, cryptically and ambiguously presented notions about the world, rejection of the social sciences and drastic questioning of the usefulness of reason are typical of both German and Argentine works of the expressionistic period. Both movements move away from the principles of realism and naturalism toward a metaphorical representation of human realities. Rather than suppress the evidence of a mediating poetic imagination, the expressionists are overtly presenting a subjective, mythified version of what life is for man. As Kasimir Edschmid said in his *Über den Expressionismus in der Literatur und die neue Dichtung,* the expressionist did not photograph, but rather had visions.[1]

Besides the evident points of coincidence between the German and Argentine movements, there exist indications of a direct and an indirect influence from the former to the latter. Jorge Luis Borges, coming of age in Europe during the years of greatest cultural upheaval, read the German expressionists in the original language. His attempts to reproduce the syntactic fragmentation and horrors-of-war theme of that poetry in Spanish reappeared in 1964, giving evidence of the link between two flowerings of expressionism.[2] Indeed, all his career has been marked by his early exposure to expressionism. He has translated Kafka, paid tribute to expressionistic authors in his own writings and urged his readers and lecture audiences to read the expressionists for themselves.

Macedonio Fernández and his friend and mentor, Ramón Gómez de la Serna, were both keenly alert to the winds of change in the literary world, since both were eager to see the demolition of the verisimilar, linear narrative. Gómez de la Serna was on hand at the emergence of the various vanguardistic movements that proliferated in early twentieth-century Europe. He was a lecturer, eccentric theorist, founder and frequenter of literary cafés and a man endlessly willing to discuss a proposed alternative to traditional literary forms.[3] Macedonio Fernández corresponded with the Spanish writer before and after the latter came to Argentina. Although often characterized as a solitary type, Macedonio

Fernández kept in contact with a number of clever, original and dedicatedly vanguardistic individuals.[4] Both Gómez de la Serna and Macedonio Fernández represent the cosmopolitan outlook that made Argentina a propitious place for a Latin American version of expressionism to emerge. Something of the same openness to change can be seen even in the literary career of Roberto Arlt. A look through Arlt's journalistic notes reveals his acquaintance with the work of numerous twentieth-century writers and in particular his admiration for Ramón Gómez de la Serna. Recent Arlt critics have tended to be very dubious about Arlt's image as a semi-illiterate.[5]

Although only Argentine writers are discussed here, some other Latin-American writers could also be considered as representative of expressionism. One thinks especially of the Uruguayan Horacio Quiroga (1878-1937). His writings, like those of Arlt, have often been considered rough, violent and naturalistic in a somewhat deviant way. Since more critical attention is now focused on the purposeful distortions, sophisticated modes of narration and deliberately "literary" elements in Quiroga's work, he may come to be accepted as a Latin American expressionist. Another likely candidate is the Venezuelan Arturo Uslar Pietri (b. 1906), particularly on the basis of his highly fragmented novel, Las lanzas coloradas (1931). Uslar Pietri is often associated with magical realism, a critical concept that he himself brought to the discussion of Latin American literature. The dates and innovative features of his entreguerre production, though, put him among those Latin American writers who can be considered expressionists.

This study, however, has chosen to focus on Argentine expressionists because of the close confidence between their literary innovations and, especially, because of the literary climate in which these men lived and worked. While Buenos Aires and Mexico City were the two true literary capitals of Latin America, Mexico's literary outlook at that time tended to be toward national authors and concerns. Buenos Aires, with its interest in European vanguardistic movements and its coming and going of literati between Europe and Argentina, seems the most likely spot for the appearance of what began as a European movement. Because this study is especially concerned with demonstrating the existence of a literary movement specific to a time and group of writers, it limits itself to the Argentine authors. In fact, we hope that even if the link between German and Argentine literary movements should fail to satisfy the reader of this study, he will accept that there was something in Argentina between the wars that radically changed the course of twentieth-century Latin American literature. A general discarding of previous literary conventions and expectations took place, along with a search for less directly representative and less linear forms of literature. This widespread upheaval affected writers on both sides of the traditionally-made distinction between elitist and proletarian literature.

The time focus of the study precludes any extensive discussion of works written after 1940. Such a limitation had to be imposed because of considerations of space and of scope. The impact made by expressionism was so great that, while the movement itself is over, the features it pioneered are found throughout contemporary Latin American literature.

Moreover, there are good theoretical reasons for setting a
time limit on any literary "ism." René Wellek presents
these considerations in his celebrated essay on the problem
of the "ism." In "The Concept of Baroque" Wellek argues
that unless temporal boundaries are set for a literary
movement, the term used to designate that movement soon
begins to lose all meaning. He shows that characteristics
posited as typical of any movement can be found in literary
works taken from any period.[6] This study heeds Wellek's
warning and considers as expressionistic, *strictu sensu*,
only those works written during the expressionistic period.

However, it is undeniable that works of the *nueva
narrativa*, particularly those that display "magical realism,"
exhibit features of expressionism. Thus we see how lasting
and important the changes made by the expressionists were,
effecting a genuine transformation of Latin American letters.
To show this significant kinship between expressionism and
nueva narrativa, we have briefly discussed a few works of
the contemporary movement. Particularly indicative of the
correspondence is the way in which both movements question
how valid ratiocination really is in dealing with man's
problems. Both try to force readers to think in new and
unaccustomed ways about literature and in particular about
the human figure in literature. Thus the chapter on the
questioning of reason as well as the discussion of the character in the expressionistic work end with some examples
drawn from contemporary authors. The third chapter of the
study, a discussion of chaotic structure in expressionism,
does not discuss any recent works. While some contemporary
writings exhibit the haphazard, arbitrary structure typical
of Argentine expressionism--for instance, Ernesto Sabato's
chaotic 1974 work *Abaddón, el exterminador*--such dishevelment
is not really representative of the *nueva narrativa*. It is
more characteristic of contemporary authors to move toward
the creation of a complex structural design other than the
traditional linear plot. Therefore, it seems more reasonable
not to make a case for structural disorder as part of what
expressionism gave the *nueva narrativa*. Rather one might
say that expressionism, with its wild disorder, effected a
break with the previous, highly linear, notion of the structure of a literary work.

II

Having thus established the boundaries of the literature
under discussion, this study commented on three main features
of expressionism in Argentine literature. The first was the
use of literature to question how applicable man's reasoning
capacities were to the living of his life. Feelings, experiences, actions, decisions and the most basic human problems
are shown as phenomena lying outside the scope of rational
inquiry. It is suggested that man occasions himself more
confusion and grief by persisting in his attempts to submit
all occurrences to rational scrutiny, since those occurrences
may be wholly unamenable to rational analysis or remedy.

In Arlt's 1952 *El desierto entra a la ciudad* and
Discépolo's 1910 *Entre el hierro*, characters encounter difficulties that remain inaccessible to reason. Some characters become exemplary fools by their dogged attempts to

subject all matters to reasonable criteria. Their rational
discourse leads nowhere. Characters able to take an approach
that bypasses everything rational, civilized and linear are
more sympathetically depicted. While they may not be more
successful than the reason-dependent characters in dealing
with the expressionistic universe, they are more able to
understand its nature and look less like fools. In Borges's
1935 *Historia universal de la infamia*, it is the reader
whose rigorous habits of mind are ridiculed. The narrator
mimics the code of the sociological inquiry using case-study
method. The reader is thus tempted to read the work as a
principled inquiry into evil. If he does so, he will be
betrayed by the ironic narrator, who eventually disrupts the
very code he so expertly mimics. The phenomenon under discussion becomes progressively less, not more, comprehensible.
Eventually, the reader is left with a vast accumulation of
unassimilable data. The rhetorical effect is to make him
distrustful of reason and skeptical about what it can accomplish in a world such as ours.

A second key feature of expressionism is the creation
of a literary work homologous to the world as seen by the
expressionists: chaotic, fragmented, inaccessible and arbi-
trarily structured. The reader finds himself at sea amid
a profusion of data that appears insignificant. Meanwhile,
the bits of information he would most like to have are withheld from him. Typical of both Arlt's Erdosain novels and
the writings of Macedonio Fernández are tremendous fragmentation of structure, puzzling repetitions and omissions,
ambiguity about major aspects of the work and detailed
explanation of seemingly trivial points.

In both Arlt and Macedonio Fernández, the narrative
voice is an important source of confusion. The chronicler
of events who narrates the Erdosain novels is not only unreliable but often deliberately disorienting. For instance,
he attaches footnotes that state that he has lied to the
reader in the text proper. Also by means of footnotes, the
narrator tantalizes his reader by claiming to know more than
he reveals about the puzzling aspects of the plot. He pretends to withhold the story of a ten-day hiatus in the pro-
tagonist's life and the contents of a notebook that may
reveal the innermost thoughts of an enigmatic character.
Even readers who believe in the self-enclosed nature of the
work of fiction can easily believe that the narrator is depriving him of extra information about the characters. That
the narrator himself is only another fiction makes the procedure yet more irregular.

The narrative voice in Macedonio Fernández expresses
camaraderie with the reader. He endlessly assumes that the
reader will agree to the most erratic manner of elaborating
a novel. Indeed, it is presupposed that readers have been
awaiting just such a novel and only read linear, realistic
books as a way of passing the long years of waiting. Struggles with the forces of the literary establishment are
recounted with the confident expectation that the reader
will side with the innovative author, not the conventional
literati and editors. The reader thus finds himself included
in an elite made up of those who understand that a new novel
must be produced, requiring the cooperation of reader and
author. Numerous demands are then made of the reader of the

future: he must not read consecutively, must not clamor for plot development or character delineation, must not try to see a direct reflection of reality in any feature of the work. The privilege of participating in the realization of the first good novel turns out to be a very exigent one. It demands the sacrifice of much of what makes reading pleasurable to the average reader. One must suffer such erratic procedures as a series of prologues over a hundred pages in length. Most difficult, though, is the implied demand that the reader read on, knowing that the novel is leading nowhere in its circuitous manner.

In both Arlt and Macedonio, the adjustments the reader must make to the irregularly-constructed fiction and the adjustments he must make to live in a randomly-structured world are homologous. By learning to read a literary work without always having sense, order and logic, the reader learns something about how he must live in the world.

The third feature of expressionism discussed is the creation of characters who cannot be held to real-life criteria and are like real-world beings only in a very figurative way. The reader must adjust what he expects of such characters to the context in which they exist, the wildly distorted universe of expressionistic fiction. In this way he can obtain a more satisfactory reading of the work. For instance, the presentation of physical appearances in Arlt's fiction appears at first to be completely erratic. However, an examination shows that a character's physical features are typically mentioned when they attract the attention of another character or of the possessor of the characteristic. In the hypersubjective expressionistic world, it is fitting that a physical feature only really exists when someone's attention focuses on it.

Expressionistic characters cannot be held to the same standards that we use for real-life persons. For instance, Arlt's characters appear mad by the standards of this world. However, their comportment is suited not to our world, but to the disordered fictional universe of expressionism. This fictional universe is so arbitrary and so little governed by rules that sanity counts for little. An "insane" willingness to live without logic and good sense may be the best means of surviving such chaos. Indeed, the character who most overtly bypasses the civilized and sane is the character who most often accomplishes his goals.

Verisimilar characters may present us with psychological, sociological or existential insights about real human beings. Expressionistic characters comment upon reality, but in a more enigmatic, indirect fashion. They may comment on the governance of the universe, the necessity of using one's non-rational faculties or they may draw attention to the innovative nature of the work in which they appear. Arlt's Hipólita is a paradigmatically expressionistic character. She is a prostitute, and though one often finds prostitutes in naturalistic fiction, Hipólita is presented in a manner far from naturalistic. While the naturalistic prostitute must be typical of women who prostitute themselves in reality, Hipólita is utterly atypical. Her unlikely life story would be unacceptable as material for a case study, because it is too anomalous. Moreover, we never obtain a "true" image of Hipólita, but only a fluctuating, highly "mythic" image of her as perceived by two unstable men. Even a snap-shot cannot convey any objective, definitive representation of the enigmatic woman.

Hipólita's presentation is paradigmatic in two ways of the innovations represented by expressionism. First, as an antirealist version of the prostitute character, a character we associate with naturalism, she underscores expressionism's rejection of verisimilitude. As Kasimir Edschmid phrased it: "Die Welt ist da. Es wäre sinnlos, sie zu wiederholen."[7] Second, the erratic, inconsistent manner in which she is represented within the novel obliges the reader to reconsider the expectations he brings to the reading of literature and, by extension, to the perception of reality.

Through all three of these procedures there run certain common concerns. Expressionism sought to wean mankind away from its excessive dependence on everything orderly, rational and civilized. To this and it employed "Sturz und Schrei," "Aufruf und Empörung"[8] and "eruption, explosion, intensity."[9] The expressionist sought an alternative to realism and naturalism, which implicitly or overtly fostered a rationalistic notion of the world. The knowledge most worth having, expressionism maintained, was inaccessible to those who relied on scientific models for their inquiry. The most chaotic and illogical parts of man's experience were the essential ones, no matter how determined one might be not to recognize their importance. To convince readers to confront the incoherence amid which man lives, expressionist literature makes use of deliberate and purposeful structural incoherence.

ENDNOTES

1. Kasimir Edschmid, *Über den Expressionismus in der Literatur und die neue Dichtung,* cited in Walter H. Sokel, *The Writer in Extremis: Expressionism in Twentieth-Century German Literature* (Stanford: Stanford University Press, 1959), p. 32.

2. Guillermo de Torre, "Para la prehistoria ultraísta de Borges," *Hispania,* 47 (1964), 457-63. Also in *Cuadernos hispanoamericanos,* 169 (1964), 5-15.

3. See Rita Mazzatti Gardiol, *Ramón Gomez de la Serna* (New York: Twayne Publishers, 1974), pp. 21-28.

4. See, for example, a book of reminiscences by various creative people who conversed with the author, *Macedonio Fernández,* ed. Germán L. García (Buenos Aires: Carlos Pérez Editor, 1968).

5. For instance, such dubiety is expressed by David Viñas in "El escritor vacilante: Arlt, Boedo y Discépolo," in his *Literatura argentina y realidad política* (Buenos Aires: Siglo Veinte, 1971), pp. 67-73; by Adolfo Prieto in his "La fantasía y lo fantástico en Roberto Arlt," prefatory essay to Roberto Arlt, *Un relato inédito de Roberto Arlt* (Buenos Aires: Tiempo Contemporáneo, 1968); pp. 9-36 and by Noé Jitrik in "Bipolaridad en la historia de la literatura argentina," in his *Ensayos y estudios de literatura argentina* (Buenos Aires: Galerna, 1970), pp. 233-34, 236.

6. René Wellek, "The Concept of Baroque," in his *Concepts of Criticism* (New Haven: Yale University Press, 1964), pp. 82-90.

7. Kasimir Edschmid, *Über den Expressionismus in der Literatur und die neue Dichtung,* cited in Henry Hatfield, *Modern German Literature* (New York: St. Martin's Press, 1967), p. 58.

8. Kurt Pinthus, section titles employed in his anthology of expressionist poets, *Menschheitsdämmerung: Symphonie jungster Dichtung* (Berlin: Rohwolt, 1920).

9. Pinthus, introduction to *Menschheitsdämmerung,* trans. Henry Hatfield, p. 60.